The Gospel of Thomas and Christian Wisdom

STEVAN L. DAVIES

The Gospel of Thomas and Christian Wisdom

THE SEABURY PRESS | NEW YORK

1983
The Seabury Press
815 Second Avenue
New York, N.Y. 10017

BS
2860
.T52
D38
1983

Library of Congress Cataloging in Publication Data

Davies, Stevan L., 1948–
The Gospel of Thomas and Christian Wisdom.

1. Gospel of Thomas—Criticism, interpretation, etc.
I. Gospel of Thomas. English. 1983. II. Title.
BS2860.T52D38   1983   229'.8   82-18152
ISBN 0-8164-2456-X

Acknowledgments:

All biblical references are to the Revised Standard Version of the Bible. Old Testament Section, copyright © 1952; New Testament Section, First Edition, copyright © 1946; Second Edition © 1971 by Division of Christian Education of the National Council of Churches of Christ in the United States of America.

Grateful acknowledgment is made for the use of the following materials:

Excerpts from *The Gospel According to John I—XII* (*Anchor Bible*) translated and edited by Raymond Brown. Copyright © 1966 by Doubleday & Company, Inc., and Geoffrey Chapman, a division of Cassell Ltd., and reprinted by permission.

Excerpt from Kendrick Grobel, "How Gnostic is the Gospel of Thomas?" from *New Testament Studies*, Volume 8, 1962, page 9. Used by permission of Cambridge University Press.

Excerpts from *The Son of God* by Martin Hengel, © 1976 by SCM Press Ltd., London, and Fortress Press, Philadelphia. Used by permission.

Excerpts from *The Testament of Jesus* by Ernst Käsemann. Copyright © 1968 by SCM Press, Ltd. Used by permission of Fortress Press.

Excerpts from *Trajectories through Early Christianity* by H. Koester and J. Robinson. Copyright © 1971 by Fortress Press. Used by permission.

Excerpt from *Colossians and Philemon* by E. Lohse (Hermeneia Series); copyright © 1971 in the English translation by Fortress Press. Used by permission.

Excerpts from W. Meeks, "The Image of the Androgyne: Some Uses of a Symbol in Earliest Christianity," from *History of Religions*, Vol. 13, 1974: 166—167, 172, 180—181, copyright © 1974 by The University of Chicago Press. Used by permission.

Excerpts from *The Nag Hammadi Library in English*, James M. Robinson, General Editor. Copyright © 1977 by E. J. Brill, Leiden, The Netherlands. Used by permission of Harper and Row, Publishers, Inc.

Excerpt from Jonathan Z. Smith, "The Garments of Shame," from *History of Religions*, Vol. 5, 1965: pages 157–9; 167, copyright © 1965 by the University of Chicago Press. Used by permission.

Excerpts from R. McL. Wilson, *Studies in the Gospel of Thomas*, published by A. R. Mowbray & Co., 1960. Used by permission.

Excerpts from *The Wisdom of Solomon* (*Anchor Bible*) translated and edited by David Winston. Copyright © 1979 by Doubleday and Company, Inc. Reprinted by permission of the publisher.

Excerpts from G. Vermes, *The Dead Sea Scrolls in English* (Pelican Books, Second Edition, 1975) pp. 75, 92. Copyright © G. Vermes, 1962, 1965, 1968, 1975. Used by permission.

The translation of the Gospel of Thomas is used by permission of Fortress Press. Copyright © 1980 by David R. Cartlidge and David L. Dungan.

To my father,
Lawrence W. Davies

Contents

CHAPTER ONE

The Gospel of Thomas

For nineteen hundred years or so the canonical texts of the New Testament were the sole source of historically reliable knowledge concerning Jesus of Nazareth. In 1945 this circumstance changed. In that year two Egyptian peasants discovered a trove of ancient Christian texts buried in the Egyptian desert near the town of Nag Hammadi. After various adventures, well recounted in James Robinson's introduction to *The Nag Hammadi Library*, those texts became available to scholars and now exist translated into all major European languages. With a single exception those texts provide information about the development of Christian theology (particularly of the gnostic variety) rather than information about the historical Jesus of Nazareth. The single exception is the Gospel of Thomas. That document is a full Coptic translation of the collection of sayings of Jesus previously known only from fragmentary Greek papyri found in 1897 and 1903 near the Egyptian town of Oxyrhynchus.

When the Gospel of Thomas was translated into English in the late 1950's it aroused considerable excitement.[1] It contained a collection of sayings attributed to Jesus but no miracle stories and no passion narrative appeared there. We seemed to have before us a series of the sayings of Jesus of Nazareth which was a new and partially authentic source for knowledge of his teachings.

Although schemes of numbering differed, there were at least 114 sayings in the collection. Many of these sayings were only slightly different from their parallels in the canonical gospels but others were wholly new. A few of the new sayings seemed so much in accord with Jesus' known teachings that a scholarly consensus grew that they were authentic:

> 8   The Man (the Kingdom?) is like a wise fisherman who threw his net into the sea. He drew it up from the sea; it was full of small fish. The fisherman found among them a large, good fish. He threw all the small fish back into the sea; he chose the large fish without regret. He who has ears to hear, let him hear.

> 82   He who is near me is near the fire, and he who is far from me is far from the Kingdom.

> 97   The Kingdom of the [Father] is like a woman who was carrying a jar which was full of meal. While she was walking on a distant road, the handle of the jar broke; the meal spilled out behind her onto the road. She did not know; she was not aware of the accident. After she came to her house, she put the jar down; she found it empty.

> 98   The Kingdom of the Father is like a man who wanted to kill a powerful man. He drew the sword in his house, he thrust it into the wall so that he would know if his hand would stick it through. Then he killed the powerful one.

Because these sayings are new they come strangely to the ears of persons familiar since childhood with the canonical gospels. We know from those gospels that Jesus' words were regarded by his contemporaries as shocking and surprising, and we should expect that sayings of his with which we are not already familiar may be shocking and surprising to us. No doubt, of Jesus' preaching and teaching we have but a tiny fraction preserved in the canonical gospels. It is highly likely that other sayings were once recorded and were lost through the vicissitudes of time and climate.

No one believes that all the sayings in the Gospel of Thomas are authentic sayings of Jesus. As is the case with the traditions preserved in Matthew, Mark, Luke, and John, the traditions preserved in Thomas combine sayings of Jesus with the sayings of other persons that were attributed to Jesus. There is, however, a general consensus among scholars that of all the non-canonical Christian writings we possess, the Gospel of Thomas contains the most authentic record of the teachings of Jesus.

Unfortunately, almost immediately after the publication of the Gospel of Thomas, books and articles were written which dismissed Thomas as "gnostic."[2] Because of these books and articles, there has been very little discussion of Thomas during the past fifteen years. If Thomas is "gnostic" then perhaps Christians need pay little attention to it. But if it is not "gnostic" in any meaningful sense, then Christian scholarship has falsely denigrated and subsequently ignored a text of great importance.

In this book I shall first argue that in no meaningful sense is Thomas "gnostic." Then I shall show that although Thomas is by no means a systematic document, it does have a comprehensible set of ideas, which are, for the most part, drawn from the Jewish Wisdom and apocalyptic traditions. Finally, I shall place Thomas in its context in the very early church. It is a collection of sayings used to instruct newly-baptized Christians. It appears to reflect an early form of Johannine preaching and probably came into being at about the same time as the Q document (the sayings source from which many scholars believe Matthew and Luke drew much of their material). Thomas should be dated ca. A.D. 50–70.

If these conclusions are accepted, then the Gospel of Thomas can take a place in scholarship and in Christian self-understanding which it is now denied. I am less concerned that any specific conclusions I draw about the meaning of Thomas be accepted than that the text be accorded a place in the mid-first century, for only then will the question of the meaning of Thomas for Christian history be re-opened.

Almost all of the scholars who have written about the Gospel of Thomas have presumed that Thomas is "gnostic." It was presumed to be so mainly because it was discovered as part of the Nag Hammadi library, a collection of documents found buried in the sand near the town of Nag Hammadi, Egypt, in 1945.[3] The Nag Hammadi documents are in the Coptic language but all are, in the opinion of most scholars, translations from Greek originals. Prior to their burial in or about the year A.D. 350 they were probably used by monks in the nearby Pachomian monastery at Chenoboskion.[4] The Gospel of Thomas is, in the standard edition, document two of the second codex in that collection.

At least half a dozen books and many more articles appeared between 1959 and 1963 devoted to the Gospel of Thomas, and these have influenced all later scholarship. Written by reputable Christian scholars, most of these works presumed that since the Gospel of Thomas was found within a collection of texts that were mostly gnostic the Gospel itself was also gnostic. Proceeding circularly, these scholars interpreted the sayings in the Gospel of Thomas as they believed a gnostic would have interpreted them and, having done so, concluded that the Gospel was a gnostic document. We shall return to this point in detail later.

Along with this avenue of approach went another, the inquiry into the history of the sayings traditions in Thomas. This inquiry often came down to the question of whether or not Thomas was dependent upon the canonical gospels. Although some earlier authorities thought it was, later scholarship has generally abandoned this conclusion. Most scholars now agree that Thomas shows no knowledge of the canonical gospels. Gilles Quispel led the way in this regard, but his idea that Thomas was dependent instead upon the almost totally lost Gospel of the Hebrews and/or the Gospel of the Egyptians no longer finds any support in scholarly circles. Montefiore, in 1962, wrote that

> it is often the case that Thomas' divergencies from synoptic parallels can be most satisfactorily explained on the assumption that he was using a source distinct from the Synoptic Gospels. Occasionally this source seems to be superior, especially inasmuch as it seems to be free from apocalyptic imagery, allegorical interpretation, and generalizing conclusions. The hypothesis the (sic) Thomas did not use the Synoptic Gospels as a source gains strength from a comparative study of the parable's literary affinities together with an examination of the order of sayings and parables in Thomas. It is further confirmed by the attestation of some of Thomas' variants in Jewish Christian tradition. This suggests that Thomas' source may have diverged from the synoptic tradition before the gospel material had been translated from Aramaic into Greek.[5]

This point of view is now gaining increasing support. Koester in the more recent article "Gnomai Diaphoroi" quotes Montefiore and adds,

> meanwhile, some scholars have assigned a higher possibility to the derivation of the entire (or almost entire) tradition contained in the Gospel of Thomas from an independent early stage of the sayings tradition, thus returning to a confirmation of Quispel's original suggestion. It is my opinion that this view is correct.[6]

Thomas wholly lacks the redactional characteristics of material in Matthew, Luke, Mark, or John. If Thomas utilized the canonical gospels he did so with such skill that he was able to excise all redactional elements from the materials he used. I shall not attempt to prove the independence of Thomas from the canonical gospels; Thomas' independence is the consensus of scholarship in the field. I adopt this consensus conclusion.

One of the strongest indications that the Gospel of Thomas is of first century date is the presence therein of sayings of Jesus which, while paralleled in the synoptic gospels, are independent of the synoptic tradition and superior, in certain respects, to parallel versions in the synoptic tradition. I shall give just a few examples.

Montefiore finds that Thomas' Logion 65, about workers in the vineyard who slay servants sent to receive profits, is superior to the versions in all three synoptics.[7] Quispel concurs, and states that

> two eminent scholars, C.H. Dodd and J. Jeremias, vindicated the historicity of the parable. They admitted that in the course of tradition certain secondary elements had been added. But if these were removed, a reconstruction of the original parable was possible, according to them and it could very well have been spoken by Jesus himself. Dodd and Jeremias made such a reconstruction. When the Gospel of Thomas was discovered, it transpired that its version of the parable was practically identical to the hypothetical reconstruction of the scholars.[8]

Quispel concludes that the version of this parable found in Thomas is authentic and that it is taken from the Jewish Christian tradition. He adds that "it is hardly possible to deny in good faith that Thomas is independent of our canonical Gospels, unless we reject the results of critical scholarship."[9]

Montefiore favors Thomas' version of the saying on wine and wineskins, Logion 47c:

> No man drinks old wine and right away wants to drink new wine; and they do not put new wine into old wineskins lest they tear, and they do not put old wine into new wineskins lest it spoil it.

He concludes that, "according to the parallelism of Hebrew poetry (new wine/old wineskins; old wine/new wineskins), Thomas' version is to be preferred."[10] "Thomas," Montefiore writes, "preserves an earlier tradition [than do the synoptics] in his version of both the Parable of the City on a Hill (32) and the Parable of the Lampstand (33)."[11]

Koester, who believes that much of Thomas is from very early tradition, says that "in the year 1908 Emil Wendling had already proved beyond doubt that the saying in POxy. 1.6 ("No prophet is acceptable in his fatherland, and no physician performs healings among those who know him") is more primitive than the present narrative in Mark 6:1–6."[12] This saying corresponds to Thomas 31.

Wilson writes that Logion 25 "is a variant of the commandment of Matt. 22:39 (Lev. 19:17; cf. Matt. 5:43, 19:19 and parallels): Love thy brother as thy soul; keep him as the apple of thine eye. As Grant and Freedman say, this is 'purely Jewish,' and Leipoldt and Guillaumont had already drawn attention to the Semitism involved in the use of 'as thy soul' for 'as thyself.' "[13] This apparently establishes the saying in Thomas as superior to synoptic versions. However, Wilson continues: "All the Biblical passages have 'thy neighbour' but 'brother' occurs in Lev. 19:17; the one ground for hesitation over ascribing this saying to early and good tradition is that for Thomas 'thy brother,' in the words of Grant and Freedman, 'means not an Israelite or another human being, but another Gnostic.' "[14] Wilson, unfortunately, concurs with this fantastic claim.

Kendrick Grobel, in the article "How Gnostic is the Gospel of Thomas," concludes that little of Thomas, if any, is gnostic.[15] He believes that "large portions of it contain deviant and independent—in part very old and respect-worthy—tradition of a Semitic-speaking group which with increasing definiteness we can suppose to be a splinter of the Jewish Christians (perhaps with some inherited Jewish Gnosticism in their thought) probably living in Egypt during the early decades of the second century."[16] In his judgment,

> in several places Jewish subject-matter is detectable. I cannot convince myself that Thomas' "make the Sabbath a Sabbath" (27) is to be spiritualized into vapour as it is by most commentators. After all, Jewish Christians—and some Gentile Christians too?—continued literal Sabbath-observance long after they were Christian. There is also evidence in Thomas for a social concern which it would not surprise us to find among either Jews or Christians but which, so far as I am aware, is unknown among Gnostics. Usury (a Jewish topic!) is explicitly forbidden in 95: "If you have coins, do not lend at usury but give them to him from whom you shall not get them (back)," which by omitting any reference to "hope" or "expect" apparently goes beyond even Luke 6:34, 35 in enjoining generosity. Concern for one's fellow man is crystal clear in 25 (". . . protect—or: keep—him as the pupil of thine eye") and so, as I understand it, is 69b: "Blessed are they that go hungry in order that they may fill the stomach of him who desires (to be filled)." The Coptic has some ambiguities here, but I think this translation is justifiable.[17]

Grobel's short article is a refreshing oasis in scholarship on Thomas.

Koester points out that there ought to be considerable further research on the relationship between sayings in Thomas and those in the synoptics, and particularly advocates work on the collection of parables and sayings underlying Mark 4 and Matthew 13.[18] In fact, every saying from Mark 3:35 to 4:34 is in one form or another present in Thomas (Logia 35, 44, 99, 9, 62, 33,

6, 41, 21, 20, in that order), with the exception of the private explanation of the parable of the sower (Mark 4:13–20). The sayings in the special Lucan material in Luke 11:27–12:56 are especially worthy of consideration because these are "paralleled by no fewer than thirteen sayings in the Gospel of Thomas, seven of which have parallels only in Luke."[19] Koester, aware of the tendency of present-day scholars to think of Thomas only as a subsidiary source of information at best, states that "form-critical analysis should enable us to assess the parallel development of the same tradition of sayings which is preserved in both the Gospel of Thomas and the synoptic Gospels, *It is not improbable that each contains about as much primary and as much secondary material as the other*" (Emphasis added).[20] He opens here an exciting prospect of discovery. For, if nothing in Thomas can be shown to derive from the canonical gospels, we must conclude that Thomas had access to independent and equally authentic traditions.

Wisdom sayings constitute one basic category of sayings in the Gospel of Thomas. Koester places the following sayings in this category: 26, 31, 32, 33a, 33b, 34, 35, 39b, 45a, 45b, 47a, 47b, 47c, 47d, 67, 92, 93, 94.[21] He has discovered that most of these sayings are found either in the Sermon on the Mount in Matthew or in the Sermon on the Plain in Luke.

> However, if any of these wisdom sayings of Thomas with parallels in the synoptic gospels have no parallels in either Matt. 5–7 or in Luke 6 there is always a parallel in the Gospel of Mark. . . . Since no peculiarities of the editorial work of Matthew, Mark or Luke are recognizable in these proverbial sayings of Thomas, there is no reason to assume that they were drawn from the synoptic gospels. Rather, Thomas' source must have been a very primitive collection of proverbs, a collection which was incorporated in Matthew's and Luke's common source Q and thus became the basis of the materials used by Matt. 5–7 and Luke 6 for their "Sermons" and which was also known to Mark.[22]

This is interesting, for Thomas contains in addition to these wisdom sayings parables which, all agree, derive ultimately from Jesus of Nazareth: 9, 57, 63, 64, 65, 76, 96, 107, 109, at the minimum. Logia 8, 97, and 98 are also probably parables of Jesus, and there may be others in Thomas as well.

Logion 8 in Thomas begins with what appears to be a scribal error, "The Man" rather than "The Kingdom," (cf. Appendix I) and continues in a way that is typical of Jesus' parables:

> And he said, "The Man [the Kingdom?] is like a wise fisherman who threw his net into the sea. He drew it up from the sea; it was full of small fish. The fisherman found among them a large, good fish. He threw all the small fish back into the sea; he chose the large fish without regret. He who has ears to hear, let him hear."

Quispel has attempted to prove, through parallels in later Christian writings, that this is an authentic parable. But one need only turn to Matt. 13:44–50 to realize this. The first two parables given there, the parable of the treasure (Matt. 13:44; Thomas 109) for which a man sold everything he had, and the parable of the pearl (Matt. 13:45; Thomas 76) for the sake of which a merchant sold everything he had, are the same in general meaning as Thomas' parable of the large fish, for the sake of which the fisherman threw back all of the other fish that he had caught. The parable of the fish as written in Matt. 13:46–50 is replete with unmistakable Matthean redactional elements and wholly out of accord with his preceding two parables. Matthew apparently found the parables of the treasure (13:44) and the pearl (13:45–46) and the large fish (13:47–48) in a single collection, one governed by the parables' similarity in meaning. He then revised the third of these in terms of the meaning he wished to find in it. Jeremias finds that Matthew does this on various occasions, including his version of the parable of the tares among the wheat (Thomas 57; Matt. 13:24–30). Jeremias writes that Thomas' "ending is shorter than in Matthew, who, anticipating his allegorical interpretation, may have somewhat over-elaborated the separation of wheat from tares (v.30)."[23]

Thomas' version of the parable of the large fish is probably authentic in comparison to the version in Matthew. It carries the same meaning as the parables of the treasure and the pearl, that one must relinquish all else, all smaller things, for the sake of the one great thing, the Kingdom.

Thomas' version of the parable of the treasure, on the other hand, is probably not as authentic as the version in Matthew. This is due to confusion of the parable of Jesus and a rabbinic story found in Midrash Canticles, 4.12. Cerfaux first noticed this fact and Jeremias agrees that this is how the parable in Thomas gained its present form. Jeremias writes that "whereas in Matthew the parable of the Treasure in the Field describes the overwhelming joy of the finder, in the Gospel of Thomas, under the influence of the rabbinic story, the point is entirely lost." The story in Midrash Canticles is as follows:

> It [i.e., the situation described in Cant. 4.12] is like a man who inherited a place full of rubbish.
>
> The inheritor was lazy and he sold it for a ridiculously small sum.
>
> The purchaser dug therein industriously and found in it a treasure.
>
> He built therewith a great palace and passed through the bazaar with a train of slaves whom he had bought with the treasure. When the seller saw it he could have choked himself (with vexation).[24]

The parable in the Gospel of Thomas 109 is this:

> The Kingdom is like a man who had a treasure [hidden] in his field, and he did not know it. And [after] he died, he left it to his son. His son did not know, he received the field, he sold [it] and he who bought it, he went, while he was plowing, [he found] the treasure. He began to lend money at interest to [whom] he wished.

Finally, here is the parable according to Matt. 13:44:

> The Kingdom of heaven is like treasure hidden in a field, which a man found and covered up; then in his joy he goes and sells all that he has and buys the field.

In the Gospel of Thomas we do not find any evidence of tendentious revision of the parable; we find evidence of a mistake, a confusion within the process of oral transmission. In fact, the concluding line in Thomas' parable is directly contradicted by Thomas' Logion 95 "If you have money, do not lend it at interest, but give [to those] from whom you will not receive it (back again)." It is interesting, and probably significant, that the parable which appears in Thomas shows evidence of having circulated in a rabbinic milieu.

Experts on the Gospel of Thomas provide us with interesting explanations of Logion 109 based on their desire to find Thomas gnostic. Gaertner writes that the three stages in the narrative—the father, the son, and the buyer—might possibly indicate that the saying deals with reincarnation.

> There was in fact mention of reincarnation [in gnostic texts] which meant that such men as possessed a spark of light, but owing to their sins and confinement within the material world "did not learn to know the All," were reincarnated in new individuals, until they reached saving knowledge. The *Apocryphon of John* 69.9ff. states that ignorant souls are imprisoned once more after death in the bonds of bodily existence. We encounter a similar doctrine of the ignorant man's spark of light in *Pistis Sophia*, where it is said after death to be compelled to circle the world as punishment and purification, after which it is once more imprisoned in a body. It is thus possible to understand the three persons in Logion 109 on the basis of a doctrine of reincarnation.[25]

Wilson interprets the logion as follows:

> a Gnostic interpretation is not hard to discover. If the kingdom be identified with *gnosis*, the knowledge that is latent in every man, but which only the Gnostic can truly be said to possess, we have a treasure hidden from the original owner and his son (the psychic or the hylic?), awaiting the coming of the Gnostic who was able to receive it. An alternative is offered by Bauer, who with Doresse refers to the Naassene use of the parable. Like the mustard seed and also the leaven (Logion 96), the treasure is the kingdom understood in a Gnostic sense. The purchaser is Christ, who bought the field in His Incarnation, laboured in it in his Passion, and by casting off the body of flesh in His return to heaven has found the treasure.[26]

Amusing as these interpretations are they clearly have nothing at all to do with the Gospel of Thomas nor with the rabbinic story that appears therein as Logion 109.

It seems that Matthew's version of the parable of the treasure is superior to the version in Thomas. On the other hand the parable of the large fish exists in a superior version in Thomas compared to the parable in Matt. 13:47–48. Both Thomas and Matthew contain versions of the parable of the pearl (Matt. 13:45–46; Thomas 76). Given that Thomas is now in Coptic and that translation from Greek presumably brought about some changes in sentence structure, the parable of the pearl seems equally authentic in both documents.

Clearly, certain parables in Thomas which differ from those in the synoptics deserve careful attention; they may be authentic even though the authenticity of synoptic versions has never before been doubted. For example, Thomas has a version of the parable of the lost sheep, Logion 107.

> The Kingdom is like a man, a shepherd, who had a hundred sheep. One of them, which was the largest, wandered off. He left the ninety-nine; he searched for the one until he found it. After he tired himself, he said to the sheep, "I love you more than the ninety-nine."

This parable occurs also in Matt. 18:10–14 and Luke 15:3–7. The version in Matthew is

> What do you think? If a man has a hundred sheep, and one of them has gone astray, does he not leave the ninety-nine on the hills and go in search of the one that went astray? And if he finds it, truly, I say to you, he rejoices over it more than over the ninety-nine that never went astray.

Which of these versions is more authentic? Can the question be answered, or should we simply accept the more familiar version as thereby more reliable? The versions in Matthew and Luke both conclude with allegorical explanations (which therefore may have derived from Q), identifying the lost sheep with a sinful person. Possibly the allegory has caused the parable to be slightly recast. The version in Thomas contains the clause "which was the largest" describing the sheep in a way that neither synoptic parable does. This clause, however, far from destroying the claim of the parable to authenticity may increase that claim, for it places the parable of the lost sheep squarely in the pattern established by the parables of the treasure, the pearl and the large fish. In each of these four the point is that a person must dispense with lesser things (possessions, goods, small fish, ninety-nine smaller sheep) for the sake of one great thing. The concluding sentence of Thomas' lost sheep parable may be a redactional addition. The Gospel of Thomas may be permitting us to see a consistent theme in a set of parables which, except for Matthew's two at 13:44–46, appear quite differently in the synoptics. On the other hand, the parable in Thomas 107 may have been recast in light of a perceived theme which the original did not contain. I do not claim to have a final answer to these problems; I put them forward here to indicate the possibilities Thomas offers for new understanding of the teachings of Jesus.

The more one reflects on Thomas' similarity to, but independence of, synoptic sayings collections, the more curious and significant this seems. That both Thomas and the Synoptics and Q were compiled in environments where an amalgamation of wisdom sayings, proverbs and parables were thought appropriate is obvious *prima facie*. Collections of sayings as a format for preservation and development of Jesus' teachings seem to have been most prominent at a very early time, a time prior to the composition of narrative gospels. By the year A.D. 140 the Gospel of Thomas was already anachronistic and quite unlike the writings we can reliably date to that period.

James Robinson's article "*Logoi Sophon:* On the Gattung of Q" has attained almost classic status.[27] He has discovered that the gattung, or form of written tradition, of the sayings of the wise has a history reaching back to wisdom sayings collections in Egypt and Mesopotamia. Some of these collections of sayings are very old. Proverbs 22:17–24:22 derives from an Egyptian collection, the wisdom of Amen-em-Opet. Robinson demonstrates that Q had a format or gattung similar to these more ancient collections. He shows that Matthew continues this traditional format but embeds his collections of sayings into a gospel dominated by narrative. The Sermon on the Mount is a prime example of such a collection.

Thomas too has the form of *logoi sophon*. "The Gospel of Thomas," in Robinson's opinion, "falls within much the same situation of transition as do Clement, Polycarp, and Justin, when the sayings collections derived from the oral tradition were becoming dependent on the written gospels, but had not yet been entirely replaced by gospels, discourses, dialogues, and treatises."[28] This is a curious conclusion, for Thomas *is* a collection of sayings. It is not something else, as are the writings of Clement, Polycarp, and Justin, in which small collections of sayings are embedded. Robinson knows that it is unlikely that Thomas takes material from the synoptics: "even if it were the case that the Gospel of Thomas derived its sayings in large part from the canonical gospels, which is far from obvious, in any case it retained the gattung of sayings collections. With the final discontinuation of the oral transmission of Jesus' sayings, the *Sitz im Leben* of the gattung was gone; hence orthodoxy contented itself with the canonical gospels, while Gnosticism devoted itself all the more to imagery dialogues of the Resurrected with his disciples."[29] Robinson's observations are correct enough, but one must reemphasize the fact that the gattung "sayings collection" is not something Thomas retained while being something else; Thomas is a sayings collection. Presumably Thomas shares the mid-first century *Sitz im Leben* of the gattung of sayings collections.

The format of Thomas is the format of Q and of earlier collections such as are found in Proverbs. Robinson claims that "the Gospel of Thomas indicates the gnosticizing distortion of sayings that took place readily within this gattung," and that "the tendency at work in the gattung *logoi sophon* was coordinated to the trajectory from the hypostatized Sophia to the gnostic redeemer."[30] On the contrary, the gattung was serviceable in recording sayings without gnosticizing distortion from at least the time of Amen-em-Opet to at least the time of Q. Robinson does present an interesting and significant theory. It can be summarized as follows: the wisdom tradition of Judaism gave rise both

to a form of literature (*logoi sophon*) and to a concern with Sophia, the Wisdom of God, considered as a hypostasis. This form
of literature and this concern with Wisdom in a special sense
were carried over together into Christianity, and Jesus was considered by some to be both the speaker of significant logoi and
to be Wisdom. Thomas, Robinson believes, has a more developed conception of Jesus as Wisdom than does Q, even though
both collections are *logoi sophon*. Following his own theory of
trajectories, he finds that the identification of Jesus with Wisdom eventually becomes gnosticism. On the whole I agree with
this, with the single exception that I do not find Thomas to be
gnostic in any meaningful sense of the word. That it is a collection of sayings (*logoi sophon*) wherein Jesus is identified with
Wisdom more often than he is so identified in Q seems to me
to be true.

Koester comments on Robinson's theory by saying, "the Gospel of Thomas continues, even if in a modified way, the most
original gattung of the Jesus tradition—the *logoi sophon*—which,
in the canonical gospels, became acceptable to the orthodox
church only by radical critical alteration, not only of the form,
but also of the theological intention of this primitive gattung.
Such critical evaluation of the gattung, *logoi*, was achieved by
Matthew and Luke through imposing the Marcan narrative-
kerygma frame upon the sayings tradition represented by Q."[31]
Mark also did this as his parable collection in chapter four indicates. Independent collections of Jesus' sayings were a form
of written tradition quickly succeeded by narrative gospels, dialogues of the resurrected Christ, parenetic letters, apologies,
etc., some of which served as frames for sets of sayings. Thomas
was one such collection.

Koester believes that "Thomas does not use Q, but he does
represent the eastern branch of the gattung, *logoi*, the western
branch being represented by the synoptic *logoi* of Q, which was
used in western Syria by Matthew and later by Luke."[32] I
find little evidence for the hypothesis of an eastern Syrian origin of Thomas. However, Koester's hypothesis that two (or
more) Q-format documents circulated in the early church is
anything but improbable. It is naive to suppose that we possess

in the New Testament all of the writings of the first century Christian church. Those lost must far outnumber those that have survived. Judging from the diversity of the materials in the New Testament, the lost writings may have deviated substantially from those that survived. That there is material in Thomas different from what we find in the New Testament is no argument against the antiquity of Thomas; it may simply be more evidence for the diversity of the ideas present in the early church.

The evidence for a mid-first century date for Thomas is considerable, although not conclusive. Thomas had access to very early oral and, perhaps, written sayings traditions which were independent of and, occasionally, superior to traditions in the synoptics. This would probably not have been possible much later than the year A.D. 90. Are there *any* sayings of Jesus in second-century writings which are considered superior to their parallels in the synoptics? Even John and the Pastorals, the Didache, and the Letters of Clement and Ignatius seem to have no sayings superior to their synoptic parallels.

Thomas contains a substantial number of the same kinds of sayings—parables, wisdom sayings, and proverbs—that are in the collections in the synoptic gospels and in Q. Clearly, Thomas originated in a milieu and at a time where Christians wanted to preserve that kind of material. Collections of that kind of material are certainly not characteristic of second-century Christian texts.

The format of Thomas, *logoi sophon*, has a long and distinguished history in the Wisdom tradition of Judaism. It was a format used to convey Jesus' teachings which, by the later first century, was in decline. Narrative gospels, dialogues of the risen Christ, legends about the infant Jesus and the apostles, parenetic letters, theological treatises, were in the ascendancy. The *logoi sophon* format is not simply early; it seems to have been *the* earliest form of preservation of Jesus' sayings. Certainly collections of sayings were in existence before any narrative gospels were written. This is not to say that collections of miracle stories were not in circulation at a very early time, but our concern here is with sayings traditions only. If Robinson is correct, the format *logoi sophon* carried with it from the Jewish Wisdom tradition a propensity to be concerned with God's Wisdom in a special sense. Wisdom was active in creation, gave first person discourses, and was hypostatized. Many of the "gnostic" writings of the Nag Hammadi collection seem to presuppose some such background in Jewish Wisdom speculation, although those texts contain intricate mythologies of the fall and re-ascent of Sophia wholly lacking both in earlier Wisdom texts and in Thomas. This may indicate that there is a relationship in the history of ideas between Jewish Wisdom speculations and later gnosticism. This does not indicate that the early literary form of wisdom material, *logoi sophon*, was bound to have as its content the later gnostic mythology.

Many of the sayings of Jesus in Thomas are sayings typical of the Wisdom tradition: proverbs, parables and wisdom sayings most obviously. The idea of Wisdom personified as Jesus is not lacking in Thomas, as it is also not lacking in Matthew, Q, and other first-century Christian texts (e.g., 1 Cor. 1:24). This locates Thomas in the context of first-century Christian texts, not in the context of later gnostic mythology.

Thomas appears to be a document from very early times, roughly the time of Q. It has an early format; it has much early material. In some ways (in terms of Wisdom speculations) Thomas may be "later" than Q; in some ways (in terms of apocalyptic Son of Man speculations) Q may be "later" than Thomas. Koester writes that Thomas (or a source of Thomas)

> must have been a version of Q in which the apocalyptic expectation of the Son of man was missing, and in which Jesus' radicalized eschatology of the kingdom and his revelation of divine wisdom in his own words were dominant motifs. Such a version of Q is, however, not secondary but very primitive. At least Paul's debate with his opponents in 1 Corinthians seems to suggest that the wisdom theology which Paul attacked relied on this understanding of Jesus' message.[33]

Thomas may be as old as, or even older than, Q.

CHAPTER TWO

Is the Gospel
of Thomas Gnostic?

T he Gospel of Thomas' original compilation is usually dated
ca. A.D. 140 and located in Edessa in Syria. These convenient tags are, in my judgment, unproven hypotheses.
Robert McL. Wilson hints at the inadequacy of this date.

> It is worth noting that Grenfell and Hunt were inclined to
> put the Oxyrhynchus papyri, or rather the sayings contained
> therein, *not later* than 140, and that Evelyn White agreed.
> The point here is the comparative absence of Johannine allu-
> sions, which must be held to indicate either an early date or
> an area in which Johannine ideas were in the air, but the
> Fourth Gospel itself was not yet known. If Sanders is correct
> in his assessment of the influence of this Gospel in the early
> Church, the nucleus of Thomas should probably be placed
> nearer to the time of Ignatius than to that of Justin Martyr.
> (Wilson's emphasis)[1]

Ignatius wrote his letters ca. A.D. 113 and hence the date 140
should be seen as a *terminus ad quem* rather than as a date for
Thomas' origin. The reason usually, if not always, given for dating Thomas in the second century is once more the supposition
that Thomas is a gnostic document. Before examining this let us
look at the evidence for Thomas' origin in Edessa.

Three arguments in favor of this theory are summarized by
Koester.[2]

(A) In the incipit of Thomas (and only there) Thomas is called
Didymos (Greek for twin) Judas *Thomas* (Aramaic for twin). He

is Judas the twin, with the word twin present in two languages, presumably because Thomas was taken by a Greek author to be a proper name. The link between Judas and the word Thomas occurs in the Acts of Thomas, in the Abgar legend, and in a Syriac version of John 14:22 where, instead of "Judas, not Iscariot," we find "Judas Thomas." The canonical John, in three places, mentions Didymos Thomas, 11:16, 20:24, 21:2, and the Nag Hammadi document, Thomas the Contender, mentions Judas Thomas. I doubt that all of these texts can be proven to be of Syrian origin.

As Koester points out, the person called Thomas (the twin) in Aramaic had *some* other name as well. Koester plays with the idea that this name may have been Judas, brother of Jesus (Mark 6:3). Be that as it may, the independent "name" Thomas was originally accompanied by another name: So-and-so the twin (Thomas) later became Thomas the twin (Didymos) when Greek-speaking persons mistakenly identified Thomas as a proper name. One cannot then presume that Judas was necessarily added to "Thomas"; it is more likely that Judas was "the twin" rather than that so-and-so, whose name is lost, was "the twin" and that Judas was added within a Greek-speaking community to the name Thomas to which was also added an explanatory "didymos." The name Judas would have been *retained* in a Syriac-speaking environment wherein the meaning "twin" would adhere to the name Thomas. It would not necessarily or even probably have originated in such an environment.

The Syriac writings adduced as evidence for the hypothesis of the Edessene origin of the Gospel of Thomas are written as much as a century later than A.D. 140, the *terminus ad quem* of Thomas. The Acts of Thomas, for example, is usually said to have been written ca. A.D. 225. It is conceivable that the Gospel of Thomas, said to have been more influential on later Syriac writings than on later Greek or Latin writings, gave support to the use of the name Judas Thomas in the Syriac Christian tradition. This tells us nothing of the origin of Thomas, only of its later influence.

(B) Koester points out that the Gospel of Thomas was popular among the Manicheans. But the Acts of Thomas and the other apocryphal Acts of Apostles were also popular with the Manicheans, and this does not prove their Syrian or Edessene origin. In fact, only the Acts of Thomas is ever said to have originated in Syria, and this is debated. "There can be little doubt," writes Koester, "that the Gospel of Thomas came to the Manicheans from Edessa rather than Egypt."[3] Surely this is overstated. There is no evidence at all for the Edessene composition of all documents approved by the Manicheans. At most we may grant that it is likely that they used documents in circulation in Syria generally.

The Manichean use of Thomas has no bearing on the place of Thomas' origin. By the time of Mani's active ministry the Gospel of Thomas had been in existence for at least a century; indeed, it had been present in Oxyrhynchus, Egypt, for at least that long.

(C) Finally, Koester tells us that "the Gospel of Thomas was used by the author of the Acts of Thomas, which was certainly written in the Osrhoëne in the early third century A.D."[4] This may be true (the word "certainly" is overly confident) but the author of the Acts of Thomas made substantially *more* use of canonical gospels and by this logic they too must have originated in the Osrhoëne. The use of Thomas by authors writing at least eighty-five years later indicates one region of Thomas' popularity (Syria), while the discovery of fragments of Thomas indicates another region of Thomas' popularity (Egypt). Neither region can thereby be proven to be the place of Thomas' origin. We are better off admitting that we do not know the place of Thomas' origin than concluding from occasional hints and doubtful logic that Thomas derives from Edessa. Once Edessa is supposed the home of Thomas, arguments begin to be based on this supposition. Koester, for example, writes that "it would be a mistake to link the Gospel of Thomas with the Jewish-Christian circles of western Syria from which one may derive the Ebionites who used a modified Gospel of Matthew, assigned a high value to the Old Testament law, and rejected the authority of Paul, *since none of these traits was typical of Edessa.*"[5] (Emphasis added.)

We do not know where Thomas came into being. We do not

even know for certain that it was more prominent in Syria than elsewhere, for that idea seems to depend upon the preferential attention given to well-preserved Syrian "orthodox" documents over against Mediterranean "gnostic" documents preserved only fragmentarily. Thomas was known in both Syria and Egypt by the mid-second century. Let us leave it at that.

The Gospel of Thomas is occasionally said to stem from "encratites."[6] The meaning of the term "encratite" is almost as obscure as the meaning of the term "gnostic." But, in general, it is said to denote Christians who chose a life of asceticism, who regarded abstention from food and drink as indicative of and necessary for spiritual excellence, and who regarded sexual continence as a principal requirement of the Christian religion. The apocryphal Acts, the Pseudo-Clementine epistles to Virgins, and the practices and points of view of the Desert Fathers witness the ethos and existence of encratites. Thomas shares few of the tendencies definitive of such persons.

Logia 14 and 104 of the Gospel of Thomas are directed *against* the practice of fasting. No encratite could have tolerated "If you fast you will bring sin upon yourselves" (14). When Thomas does speak in favor of fasting—"Blessed are those who are hungry, so that the belly of him who hungers will be filled" (69b)—he enjoins the sharing of scanty rations rather than self-starvation.

Thomas never mentions either marriage or sexual continence, while the apocryphal Acts are replete with tales of the horrors of sexuality and of the excellence of persons who break free from marriage.[7] It is possible to read a negative view of sexuality into Thomas but the question then is of the degree of encratite orientation of the person doing the reading. Turner, for example, writes that

> One aspect of involvement in matter which the compiler (of Thomas) held in special abhorrence is the fact of sex. Saying 37 is particularly striking. "His disciples said: When wilt thou be revealed to us and when will we see thee? Jesus said: When you take off your clothes and put them under your feet as the little children and tread on them, then shall you behold the Son of the Living One and you shall not fear." This should be compared with the parable of the children in the field who restore it to its owner with a similar gesture (Saying 21). This

is probably to be interpreted as the return of the world by
the gnostic to its owner the Demiurge by self-renunciation.
Whether this gesture is intended merely as a graphic simile
or as a parabolic action must remain uncertain. The abhorrence of sex is clear on either showing.[8]

Unfortunately it is not clear at all to me. If anything, the saying
seems to signify approval of the naked human body. Thomas,
who never mentions the Demiurge or anything remotely like
the Demiurge, is by no means abhorrent of sex. He uses sexual
terminology symbolically on one occasion, Logion 22 (cf. below
pp. 127f), but otherwise tends to advocate only the renunciation
of conventional social responsibilities and regard for parents—
this in a fashion often paralleled by the synoptics. One should,
for instance, "hate his [father] and his mother in my way" (Logion 101), which is, if anything, less "encratite" than the version
in Luke (Luke 14:26) wherein one is admonished simply to hate
those persons. For reasons given in the Appendix, I do not regard Logion 114 as part of the original Gospel of Thomas but,
even if it is included, it uses sexual categories in a metaphoric
fashion unfavorable to women and no "abhorrence of sex" is implied. In any event, tendencies toward encratism have no bearing on the dating of materials in early Christianity. Theissen has
shown that social and self abnegation were important to some of
the very earliest first-century Christians.[9]

Thomas, in its aversion to fasting and lack of interest in marriage and sexual continence, contradicts encratism. Some early
Christian authors speak of "the Encratites" as a distinct sect or
theological party, but it should not be supposed that all works
with occasional ascetic traits came from a party. Stoicism and
Cynicism made asceticism widely admired, poverty made it often
practiced. But the special observances of the sectarian encratites are not reflected in the Gospel of Thomas. If Thomas is
encratite it is somewhat less so than the Q material and far less
so than the apocryphal Acts of the Apostles or the Desert Fathers.

We must now return to the question of whether Thomas is a
gnostic document. I initially thought I could prove it is not by

showing that none of the definitive traits of gnosticism is present in Thomas. To my surprise I have found that there are no certainly definitive traits of gnosticism and that, in fact, gnostic is less a descriptive term than a term of abuse. When authors who claim that Thomas is gnostic explain what they mean by gnostic (and this they rarely do), they tend to admit that Thomas has almost no gnostic characteristics.

The conclusion that Thomas is gnostic is based upon the premise that Thomas is gnostic. It was found among a collection of documents, many of them gnostic, and so it is argued Thomas must be gnostic. This procedure is followed by Gaertner, Grant and Freeman, Sommers, Turner, Wilson, and others. Wilson gives a synopsis of his method in his introduction to *Studies in the Gospel of Thomas.*

> A convenient line of approach is suggested in the views expressed by Grant, which have been already mentioned: to examine first the Gnostic element, both by way of confirming that this is a Gnostic work and also to determine the modifications which are due to Gnostic influences; then to examine the parallels to our Gospels, and finally to deal with other questions relating to the new gospel.[10]

Because this statement of method is exemplary of much of the scholarship on Thomas it deserves careful consideration.

First, the conclusion is established as premise: "to examine first the Gnostic element" presupposes that there is a gnostic element in Thomas. This premise requires the scholar then to interpret Thomas so as to "confirm that this is a Gnostic work" and to "determine the modifications which are due to Gnostic influences." The defense for this premise is simple.

> Of the general character of the text it must suffice to say for the moment that it was found in a Gnostic library and contains little or nothing which could not be adapted to a Gnostic use.[11]

The question, however, is whether that adaptational propensity was intended by the author of Thomas or invented by the scholar writing about the text. Anything can be adapted to a gnostic use, from the four canonical gospels to the letters of Paul, from the Republic of Plato (N.H.C. VI, 5) to the Tao Te Ching. This does not mean that these are gnostic documents.

Having confirmed that Thomas is a gnostic work by examining what are assumed to be gnostic elements, one should, Wilson says, "then examine the parallels to our Gospels." It will come as no surprise to learn that the scholars following this method conclude that the sayings in Thomas are more gnostic than are the parallel sayings in our gospels. The whole procedure depends on the basic premise, that Thomas' sayings are gnostic, for otherwise the conclusion that Thomas' sayings are gnostic is hard to draw.

As we have seen, the gnostic premise is based upon the fact that Thomas was found at Nag Hammadi. Were the Gospel of Mark to have been found there should we similarly have to conclude that it was gnostic? Guilt by association does not carry over to all other Nag Hammadi documents. Frederick Wisse states in his introductions to the Teachings of Sylvanus (N.H.C. VII, 4) and the Sentences of Sextus (N.H.C. XII, 1) that they cannot be considered gnostic treatises.[12] Significantly, the Sentences of Sextus and the Teachings of Sylvanus are the only two documents found at Nag Hammadi with the same literary format (a sequence of sayings) as the Gospel of Thomas. The blanket presumption that all Nag Hammadi documents are *ipso facto* gnostic is false.

Generally, scholars following the method outlined by Wilson provide for their readers examples of gnostic exegesis of Thomas both by ancient commentators and by themselves. The flaw in this method is obvious: later understandings of Thomas are not determinative in any way of the meaning of sayings in the original text. Every source used to show later gnostic exegesis of Thomas also contains examples of gnostic exegesis of such texts as the Gospels of Matthew, Mark, Luke, and John, and the letters of Paul. No one thinks such later exegesis determines the original meaning of those texts.

A few examples of this method in action should suffice. Gaertner produces a gnostic exegesis of the difficult Logion 4:

The man old in his days will not hesitate to ask a baby of seven days about the place of life, and he will live. For many who are first shall be last, and they shall become a single one.

He begins by admitting that there are elements in the saying reminiscent of New Testament texts, but quickly adds that they are less important and not essential to the interpretation of the saying. He proceeds to find similarities to the logion in the Manichean Psalm-book, in Hippolytus' writings against the Naassenes and in the Gospel of Mary which he does find essential. On the basis of these fragmentary reminiscences he proceeds to write an exegesis of his own:

> From what we have discovered from the previously quoted examples, it would seem that we can expound the Logion 4 in the following way. In the little child is the Father's kingdom, as a portion of the light. The child may represent Jesus himself, or the enlightened man, the Gnostic. The fact that it is said to be a baby, only seven days old may be taken as a symbolic expression that such an enlightened man stands in the closest possible relationship to the heavenly world—in common with the first aeon of the Valentinians, which is the Logos, "a child." The "old man" is the man who is deeply anchored in the world of matter.[13]

Gaertner follows the method outlined by Grant and Wilson. He confirms that Thomas is a gnostic work by first examining what he presumes is a gnostic element. He discerns this element by reference to later gnostic literature and presents it by writing the sort of exegesis that he thinks gnostics would have written. He overlooks the facts that Thomas does not mention a "world of matter" and says nothing of aeons at all, much less of Valentinian aeons.

Gnostic, as I have said, is often simply a word, devoid of specific content, carrying pejorative connotation; it is a polemic term. Hence, one can preface words with "gnostic" and produce what appears to be significance but is only negative judgment. Simply calling logia gnostic without further explanation is a technique of several writers on the Gospel of Thomas.

Turner, in one short part of his essay "The Gospel of Thomas, its History, Transmission and Sources" prefaces words with "gnostic" no fewer than twenty-two times. To give an example of his usage:

> It is not difficult to account for the selection of [the] material [in Thomas] on *gnostic* premises. In common with other *gnostic* documents the parables are heavily represented. Sayings of our Lord which could be held to imply a deeper teaching hidden from the ordinary believer are laid under contribution. The synoptic contrasts between Light and Darkness, Sight and Blindness come readily to hand. The *gnostic* is the man of understanding or the child who knows the kingdom. Gnosis itself is the good treasure, the good fruit or the new wine. It is the promised 'rest' and the *gnostic* is the true heir of the Gospel beatitudes. It demands an undivided allegiance. *Gnostic* no less than Gospel discipleship is at cost and may involve persecution. The *gnostic* cannot expect to be acceptable to his own kith and kin, nor will the kings and great ones of the earth be of his company. The inward way of *gnostic* mysticism can afford to dispense with ordinary religious observances. (Emphasis added.)[14]

Could not the word "Christian" be substituted for the word "gnostic" in almost every instance here? It seems in works on the Gospel of Thomas (not just those of Turner) that lack of evidence that Thomas is gnostic often leads to frequent or even obsessive repetition of the simple word "gnostic" in hopes that a claim so often reiterated will be accepted.

Astonishing claims are made about the Gospel of Thomas: for example, that "a gnostic provenance is suggested by a reversal of the order of the synoptic material," when sayings are present both in Thomas and in a synoptic gospel but in reverse order.[15] "In Saying 20 [the Parable of the Mustard Seed] the phrase 'the tilled earth' may hint at the prepared soul of the true gnostic."[16] It may . . . and then again it may hint at any of a thousand other things. Wilson follows Grant and Freeman in supposing that, since Thomas almost never uses the term "God," this indicates that "Thomas may be reserving the name 'God' for use as that of an inferior power . . . and [this] serves to confirm the Gnostic character of the book. . . ."[17] This reasoning relegates virtually all pious Jewish literature to the gnostic dustbin for, as the scholars mentioned above surely know, it was and is thought improper in Jewish circles to write the name of God. Even today "G-d" is the usage favored by traditionalist Jews. Thomas' reticence may have been Jewish in origin.

It is essential to remember, in regard to the gnostic exegesis of Thomas written by twentieth-century scholars, that such "gnostic" exegesis can be imposed upon virtually any religious document of the ancient world—and with just a bit more stretching, upon any religious document at all. One simply need identify a word with a gnostic category and explain the former with the latter. By the same method the Gospel of John or the Letter to the Colossians could be made to seem much more gnostic than Thomas.

One problem faced, sometimes quite forthrightly, by those scholars who base their books on the premise that Thomas is gnostic is that for the most part Thomas is not gnostic at all. Occasionally we find scholars giving definitions of what they think gnostic in texts, and acknowledging that Thomas lacks these characteristics.

To account for the lack of gnostic characteristics Wilson develops the astounding thesis that Thomas was designed to fool the unwary into believing it non-gnostic. His remarks are worth attention.

> The Gnosticism of this work is not pronounced. If, as will be seen, it is in its present form most readily to be understood against the background of a Gnostic milieu, the lessons it has to teach are often such as could be accepted by any Christian. No attempt is made to place the wilder fancies of Gnostic speculation on the lips of Jesus, and much that we are accustomed to look for in the light of the descriptions of the Gnostic systems provided by Irenaeus and others is here entirely absent. There is no cosmology, no procession of aeons, no pre-mundane fall, no explicit reference to a Demiurge. Much of the book indeed could be read by any orthodox Christian without suspicion, and it may perhaps not be altogether fanciful to suggest that this was part of the author's purpose, that like the Epistle of Ptolemy to Flora, the Gospel of Thomas was an instrument of Gnostic propaganda designed to lure the unsuspecting away from orthodoxy into the ranks of heresy.[18]

Note here the tone of exasperation; since it is the premise that Thomas is gnostic the fact that Thomas does not seem to be gnostic causes great difficulty. Indeed, one can only see the gnosticism of Thomas by understanding the text "against the background of a Gnostic milieu" which is, as Wilson later explains, done by presuming Thomas gnostic and then creating a gnostic exegesis for it.

Turner faces much the same problem with equal directness:

> Whatever the character of [Thomas'] sources, it is clear that it was utilized and almost certainly compiled in gnostic circles. . . . Its place in the Nag Hammadi collection puts the matter beyond reasonable doubt. . . . It must not be forgotten that, as they stand, the sayings do not contain any explicit theological context. We look in vain for some of the more obvious gnostic themes and concepts. Aeons and syzygies are conspicuous by their absence, even in the relatively undeveloped form in which the former appear in the Gospel of Truth. The All occurs but not the Pleroma. There is no explicit reference to the Demiurge, but there are a few indications that the idea was present in the compiler's mind. *It is axiomatic that the sayings must have proved readily assimilable to gnostic purposes* and in many cases a gnostic application lies close at hand. Yet if the gnostic systems may be just around the corner, they are seldom plainly in sight. . . . *The problem, however, remains of a document probably compiled and obviously used by gnostics in which many of the distinctive gnostic ideas are either completely absent or left at the level of inference.* (Emphasis added.)[19]

This is indeed a problem. The "gnostics" who wrote the Gospel of Thomas show a maddening tendency to leave gnosticism out of their document. This requires the twentieth-century Christian scholar to delve into a tremendous variety of non-canonical texts, written everywhere from Africa to Syria in the centuries between A.D. 100–400 to find bits and pieces which, showing some similarity to Thomas, reveal the gnostic bias of what is, to all appearances, not gnostic at all. This method of scholarly inquiry too often requires us to assume our conclusion before the conclusion becomes apparent.

Even Helmut Koester in his essays in the fine book *Trajectories Through Early Christianity* occasionally seems to remain in this tradition of scholarship on Thomas although he comes close, at times, to claiming that Thomas preserves the message of Jesus of Nazareth *more* authentically than any other text. He writes that

> the view that the Jesus who spoke these words was and is the Living One, and thus gives life through his words, permeates the entirety of the Thomas sayings. On this basis a direct and almost unbroken continuation of Jesus' own teaching takes place—unparalleled anywhere in the canonical tradition—and, at the same time, a further development ensues, which emphasizes even further the presence of the revelation in the word of Jesus and its consequences for the believer.
>
> Accordingly, the most conspicuous form of sayings in the Gospel of Thomas is the wisdom saying (proverb) often in metaphorical forms (*Bildworte,* etc.) and almost completely paralleled in the synoptic gospels.[20]

Several of those sayings in Thomas which are *not* paralleled in the synoptic gospels are also wisdom sayings. The form of Christian tradition in Thomas has not been, in Koester's opinion, "domesticated" through Q's later Son of Man apocalypticism, nor has it been embedded in the Pauline kerygma wherein the passion and resurrection are of central importance.[21] Might Thomas have come into being before these trends became widespread?

Koester misspeaks himself, however, when he writes in reference to Logia 8 and 76:

> It is obvious, however, that the eschatological element, only present in a very qualified sense in Jesus' original proclamation, has not been elaborated further in the Gospel of Thomas; rather, it has been altered, almost unnoticeably, in such a way that the emphasis upon the secret presence now expresses a gnostic tension (the mysterious presence of the divine soul in the body) instead of an eschatological one (the secret presence of the kingdom in the world).[22]

This almost unnoticeable alteration is very easy to miss. It is hard indeed to find this tension in any of the few sayings which mention the soul and harder still to find that the soul so infrequently mentioned is both divine (a term never used by Thomas) and the key to Thomas' emphasis. Logion 112 reads:

>   Woe to the flesh which depends on the soul;
>   woe to the soul which depends on the flesh.

If ever there was an ambiguous saying it is this. In this parallel structure neither soul nor body can claim primacy.

What makes the presence of a "divine" soul in the body a gnostic notion at all? The idea was shared by virtually everyone in the ancient world. Judaism speaks of a divine spirit animating the body; is this too a result of gnostic tension? Thomas does indeed stress the secret presence of the Kingdom in the world. This emphasis is, in fact, a central point, as we shall see. But the Kingdom is inside man *and outside* (3): it is found by finding oneself (111b), *and* it is found by apprehending the Kingdom spread upon the earth (113). One simply cannot, as Koester does here, refer to Logia 8 and 76 as having been altered toward a gnostic tension concerning the mysterious presence of the divine soul in the body, when these logia have no mention whatsoever of soul or body or gnosis.

In another place Koester writes that

> the basis of the Gospel of Thomas is a sayings collection which is more primitive than the canonical gospels, even though its basic principle is not related to the creed of the passion and resurrection. Its principle is nonetheless theological. Faith is understood as belief in Jesus' words, a belief which makes what Jesus proclaimed present and real for the believer. The catalyst which has caused the crystallization of these sayings into a "gospel" is the view that the kingdom is uniquely present in Jesus' eschatological preaching and that eternal wisdom about man's true self is disclosed in his words. The gnostic proclivity of this concept needs no further elaboration.[23]

Well, yes it does. The idea that interest in the nature of man's true self has *ipso facto* a gnostic proclivity automatically renders virtually any religion or philosophy, ancient or modern, "gnostic" or "pre-gnostic" or "gnosticizing." The only places where Thomas echoes the ancient theme of "know thyself" are Logia 3b, 67, and 111b. The first will be considered in detail below; the second may not reflect that theme at all (cf. Lambdin's translation in *The Nag Hammadi Library*) or, if it does so, it does so obscurely; the third may well be a scribal gloss introduced by the phrase "because Jesus said . . ."

The idea that the Kingdom is present *uniquely* in Jesus' preaching is certainly not Thomas'; although it *is* present there, it is also present within persons (3b), upon the earth (113), at the time of the beginning (18), buried in a field (109), and so forth. The hidden reality of the Kingdom is surely present in Thomas. But its discovery is not dependent solely upon the deciphering of Jesus' enigmatic statements. It is available to any who apprehend it. Naturally, because Thomas is composed of sayings, sayings are stressed in the prologue to the text and the saying numbered 1. But these introductory comments do not define exclusively the single theme of the document. Jesus intended to help people find the Kingdom but his sayings are not to be in and of themselves the *sine qua non* of the discovery of the Kingdom. The sayings point toward the Kingdom but are not themselves the Kingdom. The finger pointing toward the moon is not the moon.

The question in Thomas is not of assenting to certain traditional assertions about the Kingdom but of ascertaining the Kingdom itself. Here is the crux: is the Kingdom present for one who has faith enough to believe Jesus' words or for one who "finds" the Kingdom itself? Thomas never mentions the former and insists on the latter. Thomas is concerned with the interpretation (*hermeneia* in Logion 1) of the sayings of Jesus but not simply for the sake of understanding them or having faith in them. He is interested in the interpretation as it will aid in finding the Kingdom within and outside oneself, that Kingdom which 113 claims is spread upon the earth. It is more correct to say that Thomas' Logion 1 is "hermeneutic" than that it is "gnostic."

James Robinson writes, with particular reference to Thomas, that

> the personified Wisdom of Old Testament wisdom literature developed into the gnostic redeemer myth, especially as it identified Jesus with that redeemer, and thus understood Jesus as bringer of the secret redemptive gnosis or logoi.[24]

This sentence requires some unpacking. For one thing, documents which may perhaps be called gnostic (i.e., the Apocryphon of John, the Hypostasis of the Archons, the Tripartite

Tractate, etc.) probably do have one of their many roots in the personified Wisdom of the Old Testament. However, if identification of Jesus with this personified Wisdom is definitive of gnosticism, then elements of Colossians, John, Q, the Gospel of Matthew, First Corinthians, etc., are gnostic. The idea that Jesus brought a redemptive "mystery" is Mark's in 4:11; something similar may be present as sayings with hidden meanings in Thomas but this is stated only in the prologue.

The premise that Thomas is gnostic was less widely accepted by the time Koester and Robinson wrote. They recognize that one cannot defend the interpretation of a text by the adaptations and uses made of it later and that therefore the mass of scholarship interpreting Thomas by reference to a wide range of later gnostic, encratite and Manichean writings has little if any relevance. Nevertheless, they seem unwilling to give up the last vestiges of "proof" for the gnosticism of Thomas and therefore focus on traces here and there of a soul-body dichotomy and of an interest in self-knowledge, which are treated as though definitive of a gnosticism permeating the document. But in such matters Thomas is not gnostic; it is simply a document reflecting patterns of thought widespread in the ancient world.

The definition of "gnostic" has been considered for some time to be an important problem. One definition, devised by the Messina colloquium, is "knowledge of mysteries which is reserved for an elite," which will nicely cover everything from Mark 4:11 to the Eleusinian mysteries, the Pistis Sophia and the Shriners.[25] More precise definitions stress the characteristic traits of gnosticism, such as the concept that the world was created by a demonic demiurge, that Sophia the Wisdom of God fell through her own error, and that the cosmos is dominated by a heirarchy of inimical aeons. Such definitions are useful, and delimit the gnostic phenomenon, but as Wilson and Turner admit the Gospel of Thomas has no such gnostic traits.

As it is most commonly used today, "gnostic" in the language of scholarship does not so much describe a sect or set of ideas as pronounce upon the orthodoxy or acceptability of certain texts over against others. The term "gnostic" often provides a counterpart to such terms as "canonical," "sub-apostolic," and "patristic." Valentinus, Marcion, the Mandaeans, the Manicheans, and the Gospel of Thomas are called "gnostic" not because they share a clear set of ideas but because they fail to appear in the ranks of those texts which have been considered acceptable by the later church. Arguments as to whether one or another theologian is "gnostic" or "patristic" are arguments as to whether their ideas have been regarded as acceptable or unacceptable to the later church. As the term "heresy" became one which scholars decided not to use, the term "gnostic" has come to serve as a substitute.

The question of what "gnostic" means stemmed from my inquiry into the date of the Gospel of Thomas. That text was written no later than A.D. 140; indeed, it was written before that date and the question is how long before? Arguments for an early or mid-second century date are based entirely (to the best of my knowledge) on the idea that since Thomas is gnostic it must necessarily be a second-century text. If Thomas cannot be said to be gnostic in any meaningful sense, its date may be considerably earlier than A.D. 140. It may well have been written in the mid-first century.

Because of its position in what is destined to become a standard reference, Helmut Koester's brief introductory essay to the Gospel of Thomas as translated by Thomas Lambdin in *The Nag Hammadi Library* requires consideration.[26] Koester first gives a brief description of the document and states that in his judgment the sayings in Thomas which have parallels in the synoptics are either more primitive than their synoptic parallels or are developments from more primitive sayings. He believes, however, that "the influence of Gnostic theology is clearly present in the *Gospel of Thomas*. . . ."[27] In a few sentences he sketches his reasons for this belief. Thomas, he claims, contains the idea that fundamental religious experience is "recognition of one's divine identity," and "recognition of one's origin (the light) and destiny (the repose)."[28] It is somewhat doubtful that one can specify these infrequently mentioned motifs as the fundamental religious experience in Thomas, but insofar as they are present there they follow lines set up in Qumran and by the Wisdom tradition (as shall be argued below). These lines lead ultimately to Johannine Christianity. One need only to turn to John 1:1–5 and 8:2 to find an idea of Jesus who is both the origin of the world and the light of the world. In Hebrews 3:7– 4:12 rest or repose is practically synonymous with salvation and the highest destiny of mankind. Further, rest is explicitly offered in a passage of Thomas' (90) which most authorities regard as definitely deriving from the Wisdom tradition and which is found in similar form in Matthew 11:28–29, "Come to me, all who labor and are heavy laden, and I will give you rest. Take my yoke upon you, and learn from me; for I am gentle and lowly in heart and you will find rest for your souls." The version in Thomas reads, "Come to me because my yoke is easy and my mastery is gentle and you will find your rest." This is not gnosticism.

Koester concludes his comments by writing that "in order to return to one's origin, the disciple is to become separate from the world by 'stripping off' the fleshly garment and 'passing by' the present corruptible existence. . . ."[29] The passages referred to here can only be 21a and 37 for "stripping off" and 42 for "passing by." The former sayings do not mention "flesh" at all. The allegorical reading "fleshly garment" is an interpretation of the text, in a gnostic manner, by Koester which interpretation is used to confirm the gnostic nature of the text. The idea is foreign to the text as it stands. In regards to " 'passing by' the present corruptible existence," as evidence for a gnostic Thomas, it will suffice to quote the relevant passage in its entirety: (42) Jesus said, "Be wanderers," or, alternatively, be itinerants, or be passers-by. If any comment can be made on this shortest of all Jesus' recorded sayings it is that some connection may exist between it and Luke 10:3 wherein his itinerant disciples are instructed to, "Go your way." As Luke 10:8 appears in Thomas as 14b this connection may not be entirely superficial.

Earlier in this book we surveyed some, but by no means all, of the sayings in Thomas which are paralleled in the synoptics. At least half of the sayings in Thomas have synoptic parallels. What, however, are we to do with Thomas' sayings which are not paralleled in the synoptics? Do they demand a late date for Thomas as a whole while permitting an early date, contemporary with or earlier than Q, for hypothetical sources of Thomas? We shall see that they do not, but to do this will require us to analyze a sample of those enigmatic non-synoptic sayings. Most of these sayings can be explicated through reference to Jewish and Christian materials of the first century and before. We need never resort to late or gnostic texts to explicate the Gospel of Thomas.

CHAPTER THREE

Wisdom and Thomas

In this chapter and the next I shall try to clarify the basic underlying modes of thought present in the Gospel of Thomas. I shall do this first by considering the set of ideas within Thomas itself through the use of logia to comment upon logia and, second, by situating Thomas' ideas in relation to the Judaism of the intertestamental period (including, of course, texts written at an earlier date but in use during that period). I adopt the premise that Thomas contains a set of comprehensible ideas.

Thomas' logia are divided by modern editors on the basis of the words "Jesus said," or "His disciples said to him," and similar phrases. This is convenient, but Thomas contains many more sayings than the 114 usually numbered and it will not infrequently be necessary to refer to logia as, for example, 3a and 3b when two conjoined sayings have been given but one number. For convenience I shall refer to "Thomas" as a person and author instead of employing the more awkward "author or editor of these sayings," just as one might refer to "Matthew" as the author of the book bearing that name.

The first logion introduced by "Jesus said," is 2: "The one who seeks must not cease seeking until he finds, and when he finds, he shall be troubled, and if he is troubled, he will marvel, and he will rule over all things" (Oxy. 654 adds "and reigning he will have rest"). The motif of seeking and finding is very frequently encountered in the Gospel of Thomas: 38, "There will be days when you will seek me, and you will not find me"; 92, "Search and you will find . . ."; 94, "He who searches, will find. . . ." The motif underlies parable 107, "he searched for the one (sheep) until he found it," and is reflected in such sayings as 76 about the merchant who "found a pearl" and the appended saying, "you also must seek for the treasure which does not perish. . . ." It occurs in such enigmatic logia as 80, "He who has known the world has found the body, but he who has found the body, the world is not worthy of him"; 49, "Blessed are the solitary and the chosen, because you will find the Kingdom . . ."; 27, "If you do not fast (in respect to) the world, you will not find the Kingdom"; and 24, "Show us the place where you are, for it is necessary for us to seek it." The theme of seeking and finding underlies much of Thomas and constitutes one of its most obvious unifying themes.

Logion 2 is not, therefore, randomly placed at the beginning of the Gospel of Thomas; it is the definite expression of a theme permeating and unifying the whole text. The theme of seeking and finding is also one of the most common of all motifs in Wisdom literature; Ben Sirach, at the beginning of a distinct unit of material writes, "My son, from your youth up choose instruction, and until you are old you will keep finding wisdom" (6:18). He begins another unit of material with the statement that "Wisdom exalts her sons and gives help to those who seek her. Whoever loves her loves life, and those who seek her early will be filled with joy" (4:11). This theme can be expressed pessimistically or optimistically or both ways in a single text; a Wisdom poem found at Qumran (4Q 185) contains both the line, "they shall seek him but shall not find him," and the line, "seek it and find it, grasp it and possess it! With it is length of days. . . ." In Proverbs, Wisdom says, "I love those who love me, and those who seek me diligently find me" (8:17), as well as "they will seek me diligently but will not find me" (1:28).

Koheleth writes, "I turned my mind to know and to search out and to seek wisdom and the sum of things. . . . Behold, this is what I found, says the Preacher, adding one thing to another to find the sum, which my mind has sought repeatedly, but I have not found" (7:25,28). Thomas Logion 2 and the other seeking and finding sayings associated with it have a background which is solidly within the Wisdom tradition.

This is not a simple convergence of terminology. Thomas Logion 38, "There will be days when you will seek me, and you will not find me," is derived directly from Prov. 1:28 (quoted above). It is significant that Thomas Logion 2, the first of the sayings of Jesus, holds that initial position. A unit of material in Ben Sirach begins the same way, with reference to seeking, "While I was still young, before I went on my travels, I sought wisdom openly in my prayer. Before the temple I asked for her, and I will search for her to the last" (51:13–14). The Wisdom of Solomon also uses seeking and finding sayings as introductions:

> Love righteousness, you rulers of the earth, think of the Lord with uprightness, and seek him with sincerity of heart; because he is found by those who do not put him to the test and manifests himself to those who do not distrust him. (1:1–2)

The second major section of the Wisdom of Solomon begins at 6:1 with a series of introductory sentences in which the author describes his audiences. Having done so, he begins his discourse:

> Wisdom is radiant and unfading, and she is easily discerned by those who love her, and is found by those who seek her. She hastens to make herself known to those who desire her. He who rises early to seek her will have no difficulty, for he will find her sitting at his gates. (6:12–14)

The author of the Wisdom of Solomon, in introducing his material with the admonition to seek and to find, stands in a tradition where that theme is common and important. Thomas stands squarely in that tradition as well.

We can see, then, that not only is the general format of the Gospel of Thomas *logoi sophon*, and therefore implicitly within the Wisdom tradition, but also that the first saying in Thomas introduced by "Jesus said" is typical of introductory sayings in later Wisdom literature. There are other sections of Thomas which are similarly introduced (see Appendix I). Thomas' major theme of seeking and finding is common throughout the Wisdom tradition. Unless there is good evidence to the contrary, when the Gospel of Thomas logia speak of seeking and finding, the quest and discovery will probably be of Wisdom, the Wisdom of God.

Logion 2 states that "finding" results in the following conditions: being troubled, marveling, ruling, and (Oxy. 654) rest. The first two of these, being troubled and marveling, have no overt theological overtones, although it is worth notice that one who is troubled is not enjoying the *instantaneous* awakening and *immediate* recognition and joy that are a prominent motif in the Gospel of Truth and related literature.

"Rest" and "reign" are theologically loaded terms. Rest, *anapausis,* is used in the Wisdom of Solomon to describe the condition of the righteous man after death: "But the righteous man, though he die early, will be at rest" (4:7). Immortality is the reward of the righteous man in the Wisdom of Solomon; in reference to Wisdom its author writes "because of her I shall have immortality . . . when I enter my house, I shall find rest with her" (8:13,16). And further, "but the souls of the righteous are in the hand of God, and no torment will ever touch them. In the eyes of the foolish they seemed to have died, and their departure was thought to be an affliction, and their going from us to be their destruction; but they are at peace *(anapausis).* For though in the sight of men they were punished, their hope is full of immortality" (3:1–4). The parallel structure in these passages implies that rest and immortality are equivalent terms.

Ben Sirach also regards rest as a reward of Wisdom, "for at last you will find the rest *(anapausin)* she gives" (7:28). Further, in Ben Sirach, we find a passage (reminiscent of Matt. 11:29–30 which is parallel to Thomas 90) related to rest, "Put your neck under the yoke, and let your souls receive instruction; it is to be found close by. See with your eyes that I have labored little and found for myself much rest" (51:26–27). The occurrence of the word "rest" in Logion 2 is entirely in accord with this tradition. Because Logion 2 follows upon Logion 1, this situates the Gospel of Thomas, in respect to the conjunction of immortality and rest, in the thought-world of the Jewish Wisdom tradition. "He who finds me," says Wisdom in Proverbs, "finds life" (8:35) and in a passage similar to Thomas 1 and 2 we read in Proverbs, "My son, be attentive to my words; incline your ear to my sayings. Let them not escape from your sight; keep them in your heart. For they are life to him who finds them, and healing to all his flesh" (4:20–22).

The idea that one who finds Wisdom will "reign" is also common in the Wisdom tradition. Ben Sirach, for instance, says that "her fetters will become for you a strong protection, and her collar a glorious robe. Her yoke is a golden ornament, and her bonds are a cord of blue. You will wear her like a glorious robe, and put her on like a crown of gladness" (7:29–31). "It is the glory of God," begins a saying in Proverbs, "to conceal things, but the glory of kings is to search things out" (25:2). For king we may, presumably, read "the wise," for it was an ideal of the Wisdom tradition that the wise man should try to discern hidden truth. An author of proverbs writes, "if you seek it like silver and search for it as for hidden treasures; then you will understand the fear of the Lord and find the knowledge of God. For the Lord gives wisdom . . ." (2:4–6). Ben Sirach says: "hidden wisdom and unseen treasure, what advantage is there in either of them?" (41:14). It is "the glory of kings" to find this treasure, thus to become rich and thus to reign.

In the Wisdom of Solomon the ideas of reigning and immortality are combined:

> The beginning of wisdom is the most sincere desire for instruction, and concern for instruction is love of her, and love of her is the keeping of her laws, and giving heed to her laws is assurance of immortality, and immortality brings one near to God; so the desire for wisdom leads to a kingdom. (6:17–20)

We need not read too much into the idea that the wise shall reign, although this may have given rise to Thomas' theme that discovery of Wisdom is the discovery of the Kingdom. Reigning is a metaphor for one who has discovered Wisdom; it is no more to be taken literally than is the idea of the discovery of hidden Wisdom as buried treasure. It is a term used to commend Wisdom; pseudo-Solomon's book was no more written for an audience of actual kings than it was written by King Solomon.

The Gospel of Thomas Logion 2 is in essence a brief summary of some leading ideas of the Wisdom tradition especially as exemplified by the Wisdom of Solomon. One who finds Wisdom will rest and will reign.

Logion 3 of the Gospel of Thomas is very important for an understanding of the whole text. Through analysis of it we can gain insight into such key motifs as "the Kingdom," "poverty," and the possibility of being "sons of the living Father."

Logion 3 has two parts which were conjoined by the compiler of Thomas so that the second could comment on and explicate the first. We will discuss Logion 3b later; Logion 3a is as follows:

> If the ones who lead you say, "There is the kingdom, in heaven," then the birds will go first before you into heaven. If they say to you, "It is in the sea," then the fish shall go before you. Rather, the kingdom is within you and outside you. [The clause "and outside you" is missing in Oxy. Pap. 654.]

This logion has a long and complex history in Jewish written tradition. It is, in effect, a midrash on Deut. 30:10–15 which reads as follows:

> This commandment which I command you this day is not too hard for you, neither is it far off. It is not in heaven, that you should say, "Who will go up for us to heaven, and bring it to us, that we may hear it and do it?" Neither is it beyond the sea, that you should say, "Who will go over the sea for us, and bring it to us, that we may hear it and do it?" But the word is very near you; it is in your mouth and in your heart, so that you can do it. "See, I have set before you this day life and good or death and evil."

The enigmatic reference in Thomas to something "within you" ultimately derives from this source. In Deuteronomy the "commandment" is within one's heart as well as upon one's lips. Paul wrote a midrash on this passage in Rom. 10:5–10.

> Moses writes that the man who practices the righteousness which is based on the law shall live by it. But the righteousness based on faith says, Do not say in your heart, "Who will ascend into heaven?" (that is, to bring Christ down) or "Who will descend into the abyss?" (that is, to bring Christ up from the dead). But what does it say? The word is near you, on your lips and in your heart (that is, the word of faith which

we preach); because, if you confess with your lips that Jesus is Lord and believe in your heart that God raised him from the dead, you will be saved.

Although the Pauline interpretation here is utterly distinct from the interpretation in Thomas, Paul's midrash is evidence for very early Christian interest in this passage.

The commandment of which Deuteronomy speaks is said to govern the choice between life and death, good and evil. What is this commandment? Apparently it is both obedience to the statutes of the law and turning back to the Lord God. That this is a matter of life and death is as explicit in the Deuteronomy passage as it is in Logion 1 of Thomas.

The passage in Thomas 3a does not stem directly from a reading of Deut. 30:10-15. Rather, the logion in Thomas derives from a midrashic tradition already well developed in Wisdom circles.

The oldest surviving midrash on this passage is probably the poem added to the text of Job at Chapter 28:

> But where shall wisdom be found? And where is the place of understanding? Man does not know the way to it, and it is not found in the land of the living. The deep says, "It is not in me," and the sea says, "It is not with me." It cannot be gotten for gold, and silver cannot be weighed as its price. (28:12-15)

> Whence then comes wisdom? And where is the place of understanding? It is hid from the eyes of all living, and concealed from the birds of the air. Abaddon and Death say, "We have heard a rumor of it with our ears." God understands the way to it, and he knows its place. For he looks to the ends of the earth, and sees everything under the heavens. When he gave to the wind its weight, and meted out the waters by measure; when he made a decree for the rain, and a way for the lightning of the thunder; then he saw it and declared it; he established it and searched it out. (28:20-27)

What was called the "commandment" in Deuteronomy is here called Wisdom. Job speaks pessimistically of the possibility of finding Wisdom. This pessimism is fairly common in earlier Wisdom texts, where one often encounters the idea that Wisdom, ignored or rejected by mankind, has hidden herself (cf. Prov. 1:20–28). In Job, Wisdom is not absent from the ocean or from the heavens, but it is unrecognized by those realms. It is priceless. It has its source in God and was present at creation, which is explicitly given as the time when God fathomed the depths of Wisdom. Combined here are the ideas of Wisdom's presence at the time of creation and a present-day ignorance of Wisdom on the part of creation. According to Gerhard Von Rad,

> This wisdom is to be found somewhere in the world; it is there, but incapable of being grasped. If it were not inside the world, then [Job's] references to men digging through the earth would be meaningless. On the other hand—and this is admittedly remarkable—it is also again something separate from the works of creation. This 'wisdom,' this 'understanding' must, therefore, signify something like the 'meaning' implanted by God in creation, the divine mystery of creation.[1]

As we shall see, Thomas too has the idea that there is, upon the earth, hidden meaning which is capable of being discerned.

This tradition of midrash continues in Bar. 3:29–4:1,

> Who has gone up into heaven, and taken her, and brought her down from the clouds? Who has gone over the sea, and found her, and will buy her for pure gold? No one knows the way to her, or is concerned about the path to her. But he who knows all things knows her, he found her by his understanding. He who prepared the earth for all time filled it with four-footed creatures; he who sends forth the light and it goes, called it, and it obeyed him in fear. . . . He found the whole way to knowledge, and gave her to Jacob his servant and to Israel whom he loved.
>
> Afterward she appeared upon earth and lived among men. She is the book of the commandments of God, and the law that endures forever. All who hold her fast will live, and those who forsake her will die. Turn, O Jacob, and take her; walk toward the shining of her light.

This passage is somewhat more optimistic than the one in Job. Paul's midrash in Rom. 10:5–10 may have reference to it. Wisdom is not found by crossing the sea or going up to the heavens but is to be found on earth. Like the one in Job, this passage discusses the present existence of Wisdom in reference to that crucial time of the beginning when God first sent forth the light.

Wisdom is present as Torah where the wise and law abiding are, or so I would interpret Wisdom's living among men. In Baruch's opinion, Wisdom is Torah. Man faces a life or death decision regarding his response to this Wisdom.

Ben Sirach, who is roughly contemporary with Baruch, writes:

> All wisdom comes from the Lord and is with him for ever. The sand of the sea, the drops of rain, and the days of eternity—who can count them? The height of heaven, the breadth of the earth, the abyss and wisdom—who can search them out? Wisdom was created before all things, and prudent understanding from eternity. The root of wisdom—to whom has it been revealed? Her clever devices—who knows them? There is One who is wise, greatly to be feared, sitting upon his throne. The Lord himself created wisdom; he saw her and apportioned her, he poured her out upon all his works. She dwells with all flesh according to his gift, and he supplied her to those who love him. . . . To fear the Lord is the beginning of wisdom; she is created with the faithful in the womb. (1:1–10,14)

The same general themes are present here as in the previously quoted material. Reference to the futility of going to the heavens or across the sea has become a reference to the inability of persons to number and measure the things of creation. The presence of Wisdom at the beginning and God's knowledge of Wisdom again are stressed.

Ben Sirach regards Wisdom as given to mankind and not, as with Baruch, specifically to Israel alone. In fact, Wisdom is said here to be infused in *all* of God's works. Logion 3a of Thomas stands in this tradition but it does not use the same language. That which is not to be sought in heaven or in the sea is called "Kingdom," not "Wisdom." That which is within a person is called "Kingdom," not "Wisdom" and not "the commandment." In Thomas 113 it is Kingdom not Wisdom which is spread out upon the earth and unseen by mankind. When the hidden treasure is found, in Thomas, it is the Kingdom.

The identification of Kingdom and Wisdom is one key to the

interpretation of the Gospel of Thomas. This identification can be confirmed (as far as any such proposition can ever be confirmed) if Kingdom logia in Thomas which are otherwise obscure become comprehensible as sayings about Wisdom. The use of Kingdom for Wisdom is certainly *not* a feature of traditional Jewish Wisdom literature; it is a new move, a creative shift of the tradition. Jacob, in the Wisdom of Solomon, is shown by Wisdom "the Kingdom of God and she gave him knowledge of holy things" (10:10), but this is not yet an identification of Wisdom herself with Kingdom.

The term Kingdom carries with it apocalyptic connotations, and these are not absent from the Gospel of Thomas. The term Kingdom can imply the reign of God on earth, the arrival of the eschaton, the salvation of the elect, and a return of the initial Paradise of Adam. These ideas are not foreign to Thomas although in Thomas they are present possibilities and not future events. If Thomas is using the apocalyptic term Kingdom (with associated connotations) for Wisdom (in a context of the Wisdom tradition), then Thomas stands at the juncture of Wisdom and apocalyptic. Thomas' standpoint could be termed "realized eschatology," for the revelation of God's Wisdom and God's Kingdom are now at hand for those who can discern them.

The statement in Thomas Logion 3a that the Kingdom is within you should be interpreted in light of the material quoted above from Deuteronomy, Job, Baruch and Ben Sirach. According to Deuteronomy the commandment, which is both obedience to Torah and turning back to God, exists within the heart. It is a possibility inherent in persons which may or may not be actualized. By the time of Baruch this commandment has been identified with the Wisdom which is Torah and this dwells with the collective person Israel. Ben Sirach speaks of Wisdom in another way, as a capacity of the human mind and a force within the world akin to the Greek concept of *logos*. He also claims that persons have Wisdom created with them in their mothers' wombs. This is not, of course, to say that all human beings are inherently wise; it is to say that all have the capacity to choose to become wise and it is Wisdom within which is that capacity. One ought not look to the heavens and the seas to find Wisdom

without actualizing the capacity that is within oneself. This seems
to be the message of Thomas 3a. The second section of that
logion, 3b, correlates with this message.

Thomas 3a concludes, "the kingdom is within you and outside
you," and 3b picks up with "if you know yourselves, then you
will be known, and you will know that you are sons of the living
Father. But if you do not know yourselves, then you are in
poverty and you are poverty." This set of alternatives refers to
the choice persons have of actualizing or utilizing what is "within"
them. According to Deut. 30:10–15 one chooses life by knowing
the commandment which is within oneself. According to Ben
Sirach. Wisdom is within one from birth. Thomas, then, offers the
alternative of knowing or actualizing what is within one or fail-
ing to do so. The successful can be called sons of the living
Father, and those who fail can be said to be in poverty, indeed,
to be poverty. Poverty is, obviously, the condition of the absence of wealth; wealth, riches, and treasure are common metaphors for the presence of Wisdom. As Proverbs says, "long life
is in her right hand, in her left hand are riches and honor"
(3:16). To be poor is not to have this. A wise person has found
the Wisdom of God by means of the Wisdom created with him
in the womb; a foolish person has failed to find Wisdom despite
the Wisdom within. The demand in Thomas 3 to know oneself,
i.e., to know the Kingdom within one, means that the inherent
component of Kingdom or Wisdom within one cannot be in and
of itself sufficient for "finding"; it is a beginning, an inherent
capacity which leads "outside" as well; self-knowledge is *not* sufficient for salvation in Thomas. Nor can one find Wisdom or
Kingdom by looking outside oneself without utilizing one's given
internal capacity. The commandment, Wisdom, and the Kingdom are all said to be within; both Wisdom and the Kingdom
are also outside and this is reflected in Thomas' Logion 113,
"The Kingdom of the Father is spread out on the earth." Wisdom, according to Ben Sirach, is not only created in the womb
with human beings, it is also infused in all of God's works (1:9).
According to the Wisdom of Solomon, Wisdom "pervades and
penetrates all things" (7:24). The seeking of Wisdom, or Kingdom, begins (as in Logion 3) with discovery of what is within

one, but this does not complete the task; one must also find what is outside, one must discover that the Kingdom is spread out upon the earth, or that Wisdom is infused into all the things created by God through Wisdom. Thomas stands in the tradition of ideas Von Rad calls "the self-revelation of creation."[2]

The discovery of Wisdom or, in Thomas' terms, the Kingdom is possible in the present. Because of the activity of Wisdom in creation, the present discovery of Wisdom has direct reference to the primordial past. This complex use of time categories is reminiscent of Jesus' teachings. Helmut Koester admits that

> the Gospel of Thomas does not reveal any acquaintance with either the synoptic apocalypse or Q's Son of man expectation. It does contain, however, a number of apocalyptic sayings. The most conspicuous term in these sayings, as well as in the Gospel of Thomas as a whole, is *kingdom* (Sayings 3, 22, 27, 46, 49, 82, 107, 109, 113), or *kingdom of Heaven* (Sayings 20, 54, 114), or *kingdom of the Father* (Sayings 57, 76, 96, 97, 98, 99, 113). To be sure, these sayings in the Gospel of Thomas almost always show a tendency to emphasize the presence of the kingdom for the believer, rather than its future coming. But it is very questionable, whether such eschatology of the kingdom is a later gnostic spiritualization of early Christian apocalyptic expectation, or rather an interpretation and elaboration of Jesus' most original proclamation. . . . It is quite obvious that Thomas interprets the kingdom's presence in such a way that he eliminates the tension between present and future which characterizes Jesus' proclamation; past and future can become a unity in the present religious experience: Saying 18 "Where the beginning is, there shall be the end. Blessed is he who shall stand at the beginning, and he shall know the end and he shall not taste death."[3]

This reference to the past is in accord with Thomas' use of Kingdom for Wisdom; the passages quoted above from Job, Baruch, and Ben Sirach (and examples could be multiplied) show that discovery of Wisdom in the present was also discovery of the creative activity of Wisdom in the primordial past.

It is hard to see that Thomas has eliminated a tension present in Jesus' teachings if his proclamation emphasizes the present existence of the Kingdom for the believer; what is eliminated is

the future orientation, such as is found in the synoptic apoca-
lypse and Q's Son of Man expectations.

"Tension" is undoubtedly present in the New Testament between future orientation and present orientation. But the New
Testament is a collection of documents and sources with a wide
variety of different views on fundamental matters. There are
sources in it stressing future orientation (Mark 13, much of Q,
1 Thessalonians, etc.) and there are sources stressing present
orientation (some of Q, much of John, some of Colossians, etc.).
Jesus may have taught that the Kingdom is to come or (as I
think more likely) that the Kingdom is present. Undoubtedly
Jesus was understood differently by different people. The idea
that his teaching was characterized by a "tension" such that he
somehow taught both positions simultaneously derives from the
inability to separate New Testament teachings (where both views
are present) from the teachings of Jesus (who most probably
held one consistent view). Thomas may or may not be consistent with Jesus' original proclamation, but an absence of "tension" is certainly no evidence that it is not consistent.

Thomas' Logion 3b states that as a result of knowing oneself,
or the Kingdom within oneself, one will be known (which presumably means that one will be known by or acknowledged by
God). God will know one, and one will know oneself, to be a
"son of the living Father." This idea, that one can be known by
God as a son of the Father when one has found Wisdom, is
present in the Wisdom of Solomon. There the just and wise
man is said to be a "son of God" (5:5), and a "child of the Lord"
(2:13), and to say that "God is his Father" (2:16).

In the Gospel of Thomas one is not a "son of the living Father" without discovery or transformation of oneself. This is evident in Thomas 3b in that one who fails to do this may remain
"in poverty." Logion 3 in the Gospel of Thomas can be read as
a development of the tradition of Jewish Wisdom. The one who
is wise, who finds wisdom which is the treasure, is known as a
"son of the living Father."

There is a resemblance to the ideas of Logion 3b in Paul's
letter to the Galatians. We shall see in a later chapter that
Christian baptism is a rite of substantial importance to the Gos-

pel of Thomas. In Gal. 3:26–29 Paul gives a brief summary of his baptismal theory, including the notion that through baptismal union with Christ persons may be called "sons of God." He continues, in Gal. 4:6–9:

> And because you are sons, God has sent the Spirit of his Son into our hearts, crying, "Abba! Father!" So through God you are no longer a slave but a son, and if a son then an heir. Formerly, when you did not know God, you were in bondage to beings that by nature are no gods; but now that you have come to know God, or rather to be known by God, how can you turn back again to the weak and beggarly elemental spirits, whose slaves you want to be once more?

We should point out, at the outset, that the idea of a condition of human life wherein persons are slaves to elemental spirits is foreign to Thomas except, perhaps, for a single allusion in Logion 21. Paul in this passage claims that because of what is within one (the Spirit of God's Son), one is oneself a son. This is true also in Rom. 8:9–16, where Paul declares that one within whom God's spirit dwells is thereby a son of God, able to cry "Abba." Further, Paul claims in Galatians, one may thereby know God or, as Paul corrects himself, be known by God.

The parallel ideas are as follows:

> Paul: The Spirit dwells within you.
> Thomas: The Kingdom is within you.
> Paul: You are thereby a son of God.
> Thomas: If you know this about yourself, you know that you are sons of the living Father.
> Paul: God knows you.
> Thomas: You will be known (by God).

There may also be some connection between Paul's and Thomas' ideas of the conditions of persons not so fortunate. For Paul they are in the control of beggarly or impoverished spirits; for Thomas they are themselves in poverty.

What one knows, in Thomas, when one knows oneself is not the mythopoeic history of Sophia's fall, nor that one is a spark of God fallen into a demonically created and controlled world of matter. It is, simply, that one is a son of the living Father, that the Kingdom is both within and outside one, and that one is known by God. This is akin to the set of ideas held by Paul in reference to Christians after their baptism. The similarity with Paul can be passed off as coincidental if Thomas does not speak within a baptismal context, but if Thomas does have that context the parallel may be significant.

Another logion in the Gospel of Thomas, 50, speaks of persons who are "sons of the living Father," an expression which is certainly related to the same expression in Logion 3b. Logion 50 is complex and, in addition, partially damaged. It reads as follows:

> If they say to you, "Where did you come from?" say to them, "We come from the light, where the light came through itself. [*gloss?*] It stands [. . .] and reveals itself in their image. If they say to you, "(Who) are you?" say to them, "We are his sons and we are the chosen of the living Father." If they ask you, "What is the sign of your Father who is in you?" Say to them, "It is a movement and a rest."

This enigmatic logion seems to be a series of ritual responses. It can be understood by reference to Wisdom and apocalyptic material.

The Qumran Community Rule concludes with a poem which reads in part:

> For my light has sprung
>   from the source of His knowledge;
> my eyes have beheld His marvellous deeds,
>   and the light of my heart, the mystery to come.
> . . . .
> From the source of His righteousness
>   is my justification,
> and from His marvellous mysteries
>   is the light in my heart.
> My eyes have gazed
>   on that which is eternal,
> on wisdom concealed from men,
>   on knowledge and wise design
>   (hidden) from the sons of men;
> on a fountain of righteousness
>   and on a storehouse of power,

on a spring of glory
  (hidden) from the assembly of flesh.
God has given them to His chosen ones
  as an everlasting possession,
and has caused them to inherit
  the lot of the Holy Ones.[4]

The Community Rule, specifying what the master is to teach the "sons of light," tells him to begin as follows:

> From the God of Knowledge comes all that is and shall be. Before ever they existed He established their whole design, and when, as ordained for them, they come into being, it is in accord with His glorious design that they accomplish their task without change. The laws of all things are in His hand and He provides them with all their needs.
>
> He has created man to govern the world, and has appointed for him two spirits in which to walk until the time of His visitation: the spirits of truth and falsehood. *Those born of truth spring from a fountain of light*, but those born of falsehood spring from a source of darkness.[5] (Emphasis added.)

For the Gospel of Thomas to teach "sons and chosen of the living Father" that they have come from the light is in accord with this instruction to Qumran's "sons of light" who are God's "chosen ones." One conversant with the Rule within that community could have replied to the question, "From where have you originated?" with the answer, "We have come from a fountain of light," and to the question, "Who are you?" with the reply, "We are the sons of light and the chosen of the God of Knowledge." Within their hearts, so it is said, light resides; they have received "hidden" Wisdom concealed from other men. Their light has come from the source of God's knowledge. The Gospel of Thomas speaks similarly in Logia 50, 24, and 6:

> 24: "There is light within a man of light and he (or, it) lights the whole world. When he (or, it) does not shine, there is darkness."
> 6: "nothing is hidden that shall not be revealed, and nothing is covered that shall remain without being revealed.

In both the Gospel of Thomas and the Community Rule of Qumran we find the idea of inner light: "light within a man of light," and light within the hearts of the sons of light. This light is connected, in both documents, with the unveiling of that which is hidden.

Thomas' extraordinary freedom of expression can be seen in the fact that its ideas are couched in a number of different metaphors. The light within one and the Kingdom within one are not different; they are different metaphors for what can also be called the hidden Wisdom of God. Further, to say that the light "lights the whole world" or fails to do so is similar to the statement that "the Kingdom of the Father is spread out on the earth" to be seen by a few and unseen by others (113).

The Wisdom of Solomon echoes many of the same themes as these parts of the Community Rule and the Gospel of Thomas. Pseudo-Solomon writes:

> I prayed, and understanding was given me; I called upon God, and the spirit of wisdom came to me. (7:7) . . . [God through Wisdom] gave me unerring knowledge of what exists, to know the structure of the world and the activity of the elements; the beginning and end and middle of times. (7:17–18) . . . I *learned both what is secret and what is manifest*, for wisdom, the fashioner of all things, taught me. For in her there is a spirit that is intelligent, holy, unique, manifold, subtle, mobile, clear, unpolluted, distinct, invulnerable, loving the good, keen, irresistible, beneficent, humane, steadfast, sure, free from anxiety, all-powerful, overseeing all, and penetrating through all spirits that are intelligent and pure and most subtle. *For wisdom is more mobile than any motion; because of her pureness she pervades and penetrates all things.* For she is a breath of the power of God, and *a pure emanation of the glory of the Almighty;* therefore nothing defiled gains entrance into her. For *she is a reflection of eternal light, a spotless mirror of the working of God, and an image of his goodness.* Though she is but one, she can do all things, and while remaining in herself, she renews all things; in every generation she passes into holy souls and makes them friends of God and prophets; for God loves nothing so much as the man who lives with wisdom. For *she is more beautiful than the sun,* and excels every constellation of the stars. *Compared with the light she is found to be superior.* (7:21–29) (Emphasis added.)

This series of ideas is quite complex. Included are ideas of Wisdom's creative and ordering power, her presence in human beings and in the world through her permeation of all things, and her arrival as spirit to those who call upon her. The equation of Wisdom with light is clearly stated. She is "a reflection of eternal light," which may be what Thomas means by the light which comes from where the light came through itself. Light coming (or being established) from itself is light coming (or being established) from light. The damaged portion of Thomas, ". . . reveals itself in their image," is probably a gloss added to the original text. It may have contained the idea of the light of Wisdom being the image of the light of God, but the referent of the pronoun "their" is obscure. When light is said to come from or be established through light, however, the idea is of the light coming forth from the light of God.

The Wisdom of Solomon speaks of learning both what is hidden and what manifest (cf. Thomas Logion 6), and it seems that what is hidden is concealed in the manifest world. It speaks of Wisdom which is light entering into Holy Souls (cf. Thomas' "We come from the light where the light came through itself"), and of Wisdom which is quintessentially mobile but which gives the reward of rest (4:7, 8:13,16). Thomas' Logion 50 gives as answer to the question "What is the sign of your Father who is in you?" the reply, "It is a movement and a rest." This response may derive from ideas similar to those in the Wisdom of Solomon.

The Gospel of Thomas is not a document of the Qumran community nor is it from the hand of Pseudo-Solomon. The ideas it contains, however, are not foreign to these texts, and at times its modes of expression are quite similar. To a certain extent, Thomas seems to be a synthesis of two trends of Jewish thought which themselves are not far apart: the apocalyptic and the wisdom tradition. Similarly, the Wisdom of Solomon has strong apocalyptic overtones (cf. 5:1–23) and the Qumran community made use of Wisdom materials (cf. 4Q 184 and 4Q 185 especially).

Thomas' Logion 50 derives the status of "sons and chosen of the living Father" from the fact that these persons come from the light. There are different modes by which a person may be said to come from the light or from Wisdom, and it may be neither necessary nor useful to choose among them.

All things derive from the light at their creation. The motif of the creative influence of Wisdom is present throughout the Wisdom tradition, with its *locus classicus* at Prov. 8:22–31. By the time of the writing of the Wisdom of Solomon, Wisdom is not only said to have been active at Creation, it is said to permeate all the world, organizing and underlying all ordered phenomena. This conception is obviously similar to Stoic *logos* speculation. All that comes into being is from Wisdom; all that comes into being is permeated with Wisdom. As Wisdom is the reflection of the light of God, all things come from the light. In Thomas Logion 77 Jesus (as Wisdom) states that "I am the light which is above [all things], I am [all things]; [all things] came forth from me and [all things] reached me. Split wood, I am there; lift the stone up, you will find me there." Wisdom permeates all things; Wisdom is the light from God's light through which all things come forth. In the thought world of the Wisdom of Solomon Logion 77 would have been unambiguous and unexceptional. The convention of Wisdom speaking in the first person is, of course, well established in the Wisdom tradition (cf. Prov. 8:22–31).

David Winston, in his Anchor Bible Commentary on the Wisdom of Solomon notes:

> Since, according to the writer, Wisdom pervades the entire cosmos and yet at the same time enjoys intimacy with God (7:24, 8:1,3) it may be said that there is an aspect of God's essence in everything, including the human mind, which remains inseparable from God. The only thing comparable to this view in ancient Jewish thought is Philo's similar notion of an all-penetrating Divine Logos which reaches into each man's mind, thus converting it into an extension of the Divine Mind, albeit a very fragmentary one (*Det.* 90; *Gig.* 27; *LA* 1.37–38). Like Philo, too, the author of Wisd. evidently teaches that God created the world by means of Wisdom. Although his statement that "God made all things by his 'word' (*logo*) and through his 'wisdom' (*sophia*) formed man" (9:1–2) is in itself ambiguous, since it is by no means clear that the 'word' and 'wisdom' here refer to Logos-Sophia, the matter is, I think, settled by the description of Wisdom as "chooser of God's works" (8:4), which clearly implies that Wisdom is identical with the Divine Mind through which the Deity acts. In the light of this, the assertion that "with you is Wisdom who knows your works and was present when you created the world" (9:9)

must signify that Wisdom contains the paradigmatic patterns of all things (cf. 9:8) and serves as the instrument of their creation.[6]

If Winston correctly states the position of the author of the Wisdom of Solomon, all persons derive their origin from God through Wisdom and, indeed, claim an inherent essential kinship with Wisdom. The identity between all-penetrating Wisdom in the present and primordial creative Wisdom in the past is significant for understanding the Gospel of Thomas, as we shall see.

Wisdom comes to persons in the Wisdom of Solomon as a spirit of Wisdom. Also, in the Wisdom of Solomon, we find this passage spoken by the wicked at the eschaton about the wise and just man:

> Why has he been numbered among the sons of God? And why is his lot among the saints? So it was we who strayed from the way of truth, and the light of righteousness did not shine upon us, and the sun did not rise upon us. (5:5–6)

In this context, the one who is counted as a son of God derives his special status in part from the fact that the lamp of justice gave him light. Indeed, he could claim that he, *as a son of God,* came forth from the light. One therefore might claim to have "come from the light," meaning that one had *become* a son of the living Father without claiming always to have been such a son. Thomas' Logion 61 says, in part, that "if anyone should be the same [i.e., undivided] he will be filled with light, but if he is divided, he will be 'filled with darkness." Those who in Logion 50 claim to have come from the light, and those who in Logion 24 are said to be men of light, with light within them, need not have been born in their illuminated condition. It may well be that they achieved the status of being undivided (Logion 22 details this process), and subsequently were men of light from the light.

These various ways by which one might claim to come from the light, or come from Wisdom, should not be considered mutually exclusive. The fluidity of Thomas' language and thought

requires of the reader an equal fluidity and openness to interpretive possibilities. One may, for instance, claim to come
from the light because one actualizes possibilities inherent in
the fact that all people derive from the light of creation. Coming
from light may refer simultaneously to a present experience and
to the primordial past. The Gospel of Thomas' Logion 3 urges
one to look within and outside oneself, and so come to know
what one has been, and so know from that time onwards that
one is a son of the living Father. Thomas encourages finding
Wisdom, and consequently attaining the status of being elect
and a son of the living Father, the alternative being poverty and
darkness.

Thomas can speak of coming from the light (50), of having
light within one which one may or may not actualize (24), and
of coming into the light (11). He can speak of coming from the
Kingdom (49), having the Kingdom within one which one may
or may not actualize (3), returning to the Kingdom (49), and of
entering the Kingdom (22). In both Qumran and Wisdom literature Wisdom and light are equivalent terms. It is Thomas' peculiar trait to equate Kingdom with light and to use Kingdom
in place of the term Wisdom.

If Thomas' odd expressions are interpreted in terms of the
Wisdom tradition, especially following the Wisdom of Solomon,
they mean this: all persons come from Wisdom through her action in creation (cf. 77); all persons have Wisdom within them
which will allow them, if they utilize it, to find Wisdom (cf. 3
and 24); all things and all persons are now permeated with Wisdom (cf. 113). By virtue of these facts, some people will find
Wisdom (in the creative past *and* in the present, within themselves *and* outside of them), and those who do will be called
sons of the living Father and elect.

The repeated emphasis in Thomas on the necessity of seeking
and finding militates against predestinarian interpretations of the
terms "elect" or "chosen." It seems that the possibility of poverty or darkness is as open as the possibility of finding the treasure or having one's light illuminate the world. In Logion 28
Jesus as Wisdom says that "my soul was pained for the sons of
men because they are blind in their heart, and they do not see

that they came empty into the world; they seek to go out of the world empty." This logion does not contradict logia that speak of coming from the light and having light within, or coming from the Kingdom and having the Kingdom within. It simply expresses the contrasting position that one who has the capacity to "find" and does not do so gains nothing from the fact that he, like all other things, originates in the Kingdom/light/Wisdom. The idea that one may be "blind" in one's heart (cf. 28) seems to be a clear counterpart to the idea found in the Qumran Community Rule that one who has "light" in one's heart is one whose "eyes have gazed on that which is eternal, on Wisdom concealed from men." One who has not gazed is blind.

The concept of the "elect" found in Thomas seems to have originated in that part of the Wisdom tradition which identified Torah and Wisdom and found Torah/Wisdom only among the chosen people. Those who have Torah are the elect. In the more universalized Wisdom tradition within which Thomas stands, all those who have Wisdom are the elect. This possibility is open to all and implies no "Calvinist" theory of election.

The question is whether Thomas maintains, from his two traditions, the exclusivistic character of apocalyptic thought or the universalistic character of Hellenistic Jewish Wisdom thought. I would judge that Wisdom concerns and concepts are dominant but are frequently cast into apocalyptic terminology (men of light, the elect, the Kingdom, etc.). Thus all are born of light, potentially elect, but can choose darkness and be empty and in poverty. It is very misleading to try to reify each of Thomas' manifold expressions into a minuscule soteriology or anthropology of its own. Perhaps the best method is to employ frequently the phrase "in a way." One may then say that "in a way" all men come into the world empty, and "in a way" all come from the Kingdom and from the light. "In a way" all who find are elect, and "in a way" no one is elect in such a fashion that he can find without seeking. Thomas' position at the juncture of Wisdom and apocalyptic language means that one will search in vain for tight and absolute statements.

In Logion 113 an "apocalyptic" question is given a surprising answer:

His disciples said to him, "On what day will the Kingdom
come?" (He said,) "It will not come by expectation. They will
not say, 'Look here,' or, 'Look there,' but the Kingdom of the
Father is spread out on the earth and men do not see it."

The question stems from a future-directed eschatology. The
Kingdom is expected, and so the important question is not of
finding it, but of when it will come. The answer, however, denies a future-directed eschatology. It gives no date or sign of the
end but claims rather that the Kingdom is here already on the
earth and only awaits discovery; it is hidden but ready to be found.

If Kingdom is here meant to be the apocalyptic Kingdom with
all of its associated terrors, woes, and political transformation,
then Logion 113 is virtually incomprehensible. If Kingdom
means Wisdom, then the meaning of the logion is clear. According to the Wisdom of Solomon, the Wisdom of God is spread
out upon the earth, ready to be found, but is only present to
persons who find it. One cannot say "look here" or "look there"
about the Wisdom that "pervades and penetrates all things"
(Wisd. of Sol. 7:24), or of the Wisdom which, in the words of
Ben Sirach, is "poured out upon all (God's) works" (1:9). This
pervasive Wisdom is the Wisdom which is hidden and which
will become manifest if found (cf. Logia 5 and 6). This presence
is not a future event but a present reality.

The Logion 3a aligns this motif of Wisdom within the world
with the idea that Wisdom is within a person. The King-
dom/Wisdom is within you *and* it is outside you. These are not
two different Kingdoms, they are not two different Wisdoms,
they are two different modes of one Wisdom called Kingdom.
There is Wisdom now within human beings and now within the
world. Logion 22 says, "When you make the two one, and when
you make the inner as the outer and the outer as the inner . . .
then you shall enter   [the Kingdom]"; Thomas here requires
that one break down any ideas of differing Wisdoms: one must
have within what is spread upon the earth and find spread upon
the earth what is within.

This set of ideas is expressed in apocalyptic Kingdom language. The Kingdom of God, usually thought to be something
coming in the future, is declared to be present. It is not immi-

nent (as in, for example, 2 Esd. 7:25–33), it is already here and immanent in the world. It has a past referent as well. If the Kingdom is Wisdom, it was present in creation time just as was Wisdom. Kingdom language leads one to believe that the primordial Kingdom was prelapsarian Paradise. Wisdom was, of course, present and active in creation. This is her prototypical action. But the activity of Wisdom in the creative beginning of time has no determinate end point. The prototypical activity of Wisdom continues through her presence as the organizing principle of the world. Similarly, the present Kingdom has its prototype in Paradise.

Note this exchange in Logion 18:

> The disciples said to Jesus, "Tell us in which way our end will occur." Jesus said, "Have you found the beginning that you search for the end? In the place where the beginning is, there the end will be. Blessed is he who will stand at the beginning, and he will know the end and he will not taste death."

This gives us an idea already of the fact that one who understands the end (the Kingdom) is as Adam was in the beginning before death. As in Logion 113, the disciples ask a question about the end time (here perhaps their personal end times). The response challenges the temporal orientation of their question itself; they are not to look to the future but to the primordial past. The passage seems anti-Apocalyptic. In the passages quoted above from Job, Baruch, and Ben Sirach, the place or nature of Wisdom is given by reference to the time of creation. Similarly, the Wisdom of Solomon refers Wisdom's permeation of all things to her presence in the creation.

As Wisdom literature refers back to the time of creation to discuss the nature of Wisdom, so does Thomas (cf. Logion 77) refer back to the beginning to hint at the nature of the end, that is, the Kingdom. Käsemann thinks that the Gospel of John does something quite similar to this. He finds there the idea that "the last creation leads back to the first. The one who is the end also reveals the beginning. . . ."[7] Logion 18b reads: "Blessed is he who will stand at the beginning, and he will know the end and he will not taste death." This gives us a clue to the proper understanding of Logion 49, "Blessed are the solitary and the chosen, because you will find the Kingdom; because you come from it, you will again go there." The Kingdom was and is; Wisdom was and is. Within the Gospel of Thomas the incorrect aspiration of the disciples is their seeking a future end. Logion 18b advocates seeking for the beginning in order to find the end; Logion 49 advocates a return to the Kingdom. The idea of "returning to" the Kingdom and the idea of knowing an "end" which is in the beginning are related concepts. Both deny the actuality of the Kingdom in the future; both admit the validity of future-oriented terminology ("going to" and "end") only by relating it to past time. To return to the Kingdom implies that the Kingdom is already in existence. Indeed, to come from the Kingdom is to come from the beginning, and to know the end is to return to the Kingdom.

Logion 51 reads: "His disciples said to him, 'When will be the rest of the dead and when will the new world come?' [Their usual future-oriented question] He said to them, 'What you look for has come, but you do not know it.' " As we have seen, the present existence of the Kingdom is crucial to Thomas. Thus the disciples' question about the future date of the new world is rejected and taken to be evidence of their failure to understand. What is also present, according to this saying, is "the rest of the dead." This "rest" is an equivalent term to Kingdom, in the sense that "rest" is what one obtains when one obtains Wisdom. In a fashion reminiscent of the Gospel of John, the saying in Thomas presents the present possibility of the rest of the dead, which is to say eternal life. Immortality is not a future condition in Thomas but a present possibility contingent upon recognizing the present existence of the Kingdom. The "future" Kingdom cannot be entered by anyone who has not already come from the Kingdom by dwelling in it in the present.

To summarize the argument so far:
1) Many of the basic themes of Thomas, most obviously the theme of seeking and finding, occur also in the Jewish Wisdom tradition and in Wisdom-influenced texts from Qumran.
2) Thomas uses terminology characteristic of apocalyptic Ju-

daism at the service of ideas of the Wisdom tradition; in Thomas the word Kingdom is in many ways equivalent to the word Wisdom. The prototypical time of Wisdom (past, in creation) and the anticipated time of the Kingdom (future, at the end) are both located in the present according to Thomas.

3) Thomas advocates transformation of human existence from an inferior condition to a superior condition. The inferior human condition contains the potential to accomplish this transformation. Thomas' is not a soteriology of what is given, i.e., a "grace" soteriology, but a soteriology of what is found, i.e., a "wisdom" soteriology. The two human conditions are spoken of in various ways. Thomas can say, of the inferior condition, that while the Kingdom is within/Light is within, prior to transformation persons are empty/ in poverty/ in darkness. After transformation persons discern the Kingdom/ actualize their light/ know what is within them/ can claim to be sons of the living Father. Thomas' terminology is fluid, inexact and unsystematic. No one metaphor can be used to subsume all others. Neither is one verb of transformation primary. Thomas can speak of finding/ knowing/ shining/ seeing/ making, and so forth, as equivalent modes of transformation.

From this inexact use of language one may anticipate that Thomas derives not from a philosophical school or a theological party but from persons in need of diverse ways of expressing a non-verbal ritual experience of transformation.

CHAPTER FOUR

Image and Light

Of all the logia in Thomas perhaps the most consistently difficult to comprehend are those which refer to "the image" and to "the light." Not only are the terms image and light vague in themselves, but Thomas is capable of using either of them with two or more different meanings. In Logion 22 the same term, image, is used to denote a present state of mankind and a preferable state: when you make "an image in the place of an image, then you shall enter [the Kingdom]." Keeping in mind that example of multiple, if not careless, use we may turn to other logia in Thomas where these and related terms are employed.

Perhaps we should first examine Thomas' most enigmatic image references, Logia 83 and 84. Because 83 may be punctuated in either of two ways, and because the antecedents are not always clearly indicated by their pronouns in Coptic, two readings are possible. Cartlidge has this: "The images are manifest to the man, and the light in them is hidden in the image of the light of the Father. He will reveal himself and his image is hidden by his light." Doresse and Gaertner prefer an alternate reading, as do I:

> The images are revealed to man, and the light within them is hidden. It shall be revealed in the image of the light of the Father. And his image is hidden by his light.

Although this is not a model of clarity and precision, it enables one to discern a general pattern of thought.

To begin with, this logion has a definite context in a sequence of three logia which seem to deal with the same general subject.

84 When you see your likeness, you rejoice. But when you see your images which came into being before you, (which) do not die nor are manifest, how much you will bear!

85 Adam came into existence from a great power and a great wealth, and he was not worthy of you. For, if he had been worthy, he [would] not [have tasted] death.

The matter under discussion in these three logia has reference to Genesis 1:26–27 wherein Adam is said to have been created in the "image" and in the "likeness" of God. In early decades Christianity made use of this terminology, particularly in reference to Christ. Hengel writes that

> not only mediation at creation but also the designation of Christ as "God's image" (*eikon*) was taken over from the wisdom tradition of Greek-speaking Judaism. At the same time, this concept created associations between the pre-existent Christ and the figure of the first, heavenly Adam, the 'primal man,' who in Philo is identical with the Logos and the 'firstborn son,' though it is striking that Paul does not see Christ as the protological primal man of Gen 1 and 2, but as the heavenly eschatological Adam, who as a "life-giving spirit" overcomes death.[1]

Thomas' ideas are not identical to these. In Logion 84 images are described approvingly as unmanifest. In Logion 83 images are in an initial state of manifestation. Furthermore, in the last line of Logion 83 there appears an "image" which is unmanifest. What is intended here, apparently, is a double use of the term "image." We have seen above that Thomas can use the term in a double sense quite casually. Logion 84 implies that two possibilities are open to man, "likeness" and "image" (the latter to be preferred), and this may be related to 22 where one is urged to transform an image into an image, for it seems reasonable to presume that 22 means that when you make "an image (likeness) in the place of an image (Image), then you shall enter [the

Kingdom]." Thomas 83, however, begins with the sentence, "The images are manifest to the man, and the light in them is hidden," by which we should understand a plurality of "images" which are manifest to everyone. This condition is a starting point which can, or should be, transformed to a condition wherein the light within these images is manifest. Those manifest images are probably not the "likeness" of Logion 84 but the images which constitute the things of the world. This usage is derived from Plato's thought and was adopted by Philo. Wolfson says of Philo:

> His conception of the Logos, and of the ideas which are con-
> tained in the Logos, as created by God has led Philo to revise
> the meaning of the Platonic term image (*eikon*). In Plato the
> term image is used exclusively with reference to things in the
> visible world; ideas are not images they are patterns (*para-
> deigmata*). In Philo, indeed, the term image is still applied to
> things in the visible world, and ideas as well as the Logos are
> still described by the term pattern as well as by the term
> archetype (*archetypos*), but, unlike Plato, Philo describes the
> ideas as well as the Logos also by the term image.[2]

As the term *logos* is not used by Thomas, Philo's special use of image has no direct bearing on our concerns, but his use of image for the things of the world is significant.

At the start, then, man sees the world, which is images, with-out seeing the light within the images: "the images are manifest to the man, and the light in them is hidden." That the world can be apprehended in the mode of light or not so apprehended is apparent from Logion 24:

> There is light within a man of light and he (or, it) lights the
> whole world. When he (or, it) does not shine, there is dark-
> ness.

Light in this logion may or may not be manifest and has to do with all the world.

In Thomas 83 we read that the light within the images shall be made manifest in the image of the light of the Father; a distinction is made between the light of the Father and the im-age of that light. Thomas seems to be saying:

a. People in general are capable of seeing the images, which are the things that constitute the world.
b. These images have within them light (i.e., the image of the Father's light).
c. This light can be made manifest.
d. People have light within them (as do the other constituent things of the world), and this light too can be manifested so as to illuminate the world.
e. When people manifest the light within themselves they will apprehend the light within all the things of the world.
f. Those who fail to do this are in darkness, aware only of their likeness, and doomed to taste death.

Those who do apprehend light find, according to Logion 83, that "his image is hidden by his light." Since the image of light within things (images) has already been revealed, the "light" in this concluding line of 83 is to be distinguished from the "image of the light." Furthermore, the term "image" in this line should be distinguished from the word "images" in the first line of 83, for the "images" there begin by being revealed and are plural in number.

The image in the concluding line of 83 seems to be the "image of God" in which human beings are created; discussion of this continues in Logion 84 immediately following, where the distinction of "image" from "likeness" is stressed. When 84 refers to "your images which came into being before you" we should be reminded of the consecutive beatitudes of Logia 18b and 19a:

Blessed is he who will stand at the beginning, and he will know the end and he will not taste death.

Blessed is he who was before he was created.

These passages do not speak about pre-existent souls but about the necessity of finding oneself in the Kingdom by reference to the primordial creation. The general meaning of 83 is, then, that the images (which constitute the world) are manifest to man (all people) and the light (image of the light) is within them but hidden. Transformation of this situation is possible in such a way that the light within these images is manifested. The light is the image of the light of the Father. At this point the Image of God can be apprehended but remains unmanifested, hidden in the light of the Father. No man can see God. According to 84, people can cease to exist as a "likeness," and can "see" the still unmanifest Image of God which remains hidden in the light itself.

Things have light in them due to the mode of their creation. Logion 77a says:

> Jesus said: I am the light which is above [all things]. I am [all things]. [All things] came forth from me and all things reached me.

One of the most significant points in this passage is the equation of "I am light" with "I am all things." Light we may regard as a synonym for God's wisdom. The light within all things seems to derive from the primordial time of the origin of all things. While Thomas distinguishes in Logion 83 between the light from which all things come and the image of the light within all things, he ignores this distinction in his other statements.

Similar ideas are present in Logion 50:

> If they say to you, "Where did you come from?" say to them,
> "We come from the light, where the light came through itself.
> [gloss? . . .] It stands [. . .] and reveals itself in their image.

The referent to "their" in the concluding gloss is obscure. Gaertner suggests an emendation of the text to read, "It arose and revealed itself in *an* image," which he believes will reveal the best interpretation of this logion.[3] This belief is based on his notion that Thomas follows the scheme of the Apocryphon of John. I agree with his suggested emendation but not with his rationale for it. In fact, this emendation brings Logion 50 into accord not with the Apocryphon of John but with Logion 83, wherein the light is revealed in the image of the light of the Father.

"We come from the light," in 50 is another expression of 77's

statement that "[All things] came forth from me [the light]."
The particular mode of this "coming forth" is given in 50 as
"where the light came through itself. It stands [. . .] and reveals itself in their image." The light coming through itself is
light coming through light which, expressed differently, is the
revelation of an image of light. An image of light comes forth
from light and, according to 50, this is the place of origin of all
people or, at least, of such people as are aware of the light within
them.

To a great extent the Gospel of Thomas is engaged in giving
various metaphors for transformation: enlightening the world,
finding the Kingdom, revealing what is hidden, replacing an
image with an image, etc. All these metaphors of transformation
overlie a central view of reality which can be discerned in the
enigmatic logia about light and images. Perhaps the key can be
found in the Wisdom of Solomon, "She (Wisdom) is a reflection
of eternal light" (7:26). Thomas' view is as follows: All things
come forth from light. Because of their origin in light all things
have within them the image of the light. Human beings, therefore, derive from light and have within them the image of the
light. Ideally, human beings will be aware of the image of the
light which is both within them and within the things of the
world. This set of ideas has the additional consequence in
Thomas' thinking that human beings will apprehend the light
itself and in that way "see" the unmanifest Image of God which
is the human ideal.

Human beings begin in a mode called "likeness" which seems
to be equivalent to the initial "hiddenness" of the light within
things. This is equivalent to "darkness" (24), and, presumably,
to "emptiness" (28), "poverty" (3), and even death (85). Each of
these negative terms implies a positive contrary term, and the
movement between the members of each pair is the transformation advocated by Thomas. There can be, therefore, a very
fluid terminology in Thomas which need *not* imply a corre-
sponding complexity of ideas.

It is of crucial importance to realize that in Thomas these
various expressions of transformation *do not* proceed in only one
direction, from man to world. The light is within the world as

well as within mankind. It can be discovered in either place and
may facilitate a subsequent transformation on the other place.
What seems to be an implicit temporal sequence is more a function of the constraints of language than anything else.

Thomas is content to speak of the Kingdom spread upon the
earth, as well as of the Kingdom within mankind. It is, indeed,
within you *and* outside you. For man to discover light within
and *not* thereby light the whole world is wholly against the ideas
of Thomas. The hiddenness of the light (83) is not the same as
the nonexistence of the light; the world in its reality, as the
creation of God through light or Wisdom, is not itself in need
of transformation but it can, if apprehended properly, be the
catalyst for needed human transformation. As Thomas 3 denies
the need to search in particular places for the Kingdom, so
Thomas 113 states that the Kingdom is in all places. All things
come forth from the light; all images have light hidden within
them. Therefore, Thomas 5 can say:

> Know what is in front of your face, and what is concealed from
> you will be revealed to you. For there is nothing concealed
> which will not be manifest.

If we realize that what is hidden is light and that this shall be
revealed (83), then Logion 5 restates the proposition of 113 that
the Kingdom is spread upon the earth and is not located in the
heavens or the seas. "What is in front of your face" here should
be taken rather literally; it is what is present to anyone.

Thomas is a collection of metaphors for a single underlying
set of ideas. If these ideas are expressed in terms derived from
apocalyptic Judaism (e.g., Kingdom language), or in terms derived from Wisdom (e.g., seeking/finding and light language),
or in terms derived from the middle-Platonism which so strongly
influenced Philo and the Wisdom of Solomon (e.g., image language), there are not thereby three or more distinct and dispa-
rate sets of ideas in Thomas. Essentially Thomas' ideas are unitive, urging the finding of "light" or "Kingdom" or "image" in
both the world and the individual. Thomas seems willing to
equate cognitive unity (the hidden will be revealed) with spatial

unity (the Kingdom within and spread upon the earth) and temporal unity (in the place where the beginning is, there the end will be). The sequence 83–85 indicates that attainment of the unitive state is equivalent to "seeing" the original Image (lost by Adam) which is hidden in light. Indeed, if we follow Thomas' line of thought, this Image of God can be recaptured temporally (return to paradise, the beginning), or discerned cognitively ("seen" hidden in light), and possibly even apprehended spatially, although it is not clear how one might spatially apprehend such an Image. Nevertheless, one may anticipate such a spatial metaphor.

Thomas implies in 22 that the Image is to be restored in an embodied fashion: "when you make eyes in the place of an eye, and a hand in place of a hand, and a foot in the place of a foot, (and) an image in the place of an image, then you shall enter [the Kingdom]." Given the extraordinary fluidity of Thomas' language, and the idea of the image as a transformed body, it would be consistent for him to use spatial language in the context of restoring the Image as a transformed body. Further, given Thomas' repeated insistence that Kingdom or light is to be discerned in the things or images which constitute the world, we might expect him to compound our confusion by stating that the world as locus of light and Kingdom is also the locus of the image which is a transformed body.

An idea somewhat like this appears in various places in the ancient world. Lohse writes that

> the Stoic view of nature takes this idea of the body of the All-Divinity and conceives of the whole cosmos as being filled by the deity. Men, however, are members of this world-encompassing body which binds all things together. These conceptions also found entrance into Hellenistic Judaism so that Philo of Alexandria speaks of the world of the heavens as a uniform body over which the Logos is set as the head (Som. 1.128). *The Logos encompasses all things, he fills and defines them to their extremities* (Quaest. in Ex. 2.68). (Emphasis added.)[4]

In Christianity this conception also had a place. It seems to lie behind an early hymn in Col. 1:15–20, of which Lohse says:

The statements of the Christian confession are summarized by the hymn in the words that Christ is the head of the body. This mythological manner of conceptualization in which the cosmos appears as a body governed by its head provides the answer to man's search—man who is beset by worry and fear of the power in the world and who asks how the world can be brought to its proper order: Christ is the "head" (*kephale*) that governs the "body" (*soma*) of the cosmos; the cosmos is ruled and held together by this head. The universe is ruled and established through him alone, i.e. in him alone is salvation.[5]

Hengel quotes Philo as saying,

"Having received the divine seed, when her travail was consummated, she [Wisdom] bore the only son who is apprehended by the senses, the world which we see." Here *Jewish wisdom speculation is connected with the Platonic doctrine of creation to be found in the Timaeus.* To God the Father of the universe there corresponds *the world as son.* (Hengel's emphasis.)[6]

Thomas, as we have seen, contains in Logion 77 the idea of the light, Jesus/Wisdom, which "encompasses all things . . . fills and defines them to their extremities."

Neither head nor logos is a term predicated of Jesus in Thomas. The principal term used there is light; "body" (taken in a Stoic/Philonic sense) may be an alternative term for light in Logion 80 which reads:

He who has known the world has found the body (light?), but he who has found the body (light?), the world is not worthy of him.

Thomas, in something of the same fashion as John, uses the term "world" in two senses. First, he uses it to signify the goal of the search constantly commended in his logia. Second, he uses it to sum up those things that a person should reject. This second use is plain in Logion 27: "If you do not fast (in respect to) the world, you will not find the Kingdom." Since Thomas, in the fashion of very primitive Christianity, advocates the renunciation of family ties (see 99 and 101) and disvalues financial concerns (see 63 and 95), one may well presume that "world" in the negative sense is the world of society and of structured social obligations. It is certainly *not* the earth upon which the Kingdom of the Father is spread.

Thomas, in dividing the world into two aspects, one positively and the other negatively valued, seems to be echoing a Wisdom tradition. Von Rad writes that

> It has been correctly asserted that the division of the world into a benevolent world ruled by God and a malevolent world ruled by evil first becomes discernible in the Hellenistic Wisdom of Solomon.[7]

However, Thomas may not find the world evil at all, except in its social ramifications. Demonic powers do not appear in Thomas, unless one reads them into the "owners of the field," and "robbers" in Logion 21.

Thomas' Logion 110 is typical of his dual use of the term "world": "He who has found the world and becomes rich, let him deny the world." Becoming rich is the opposite of "poverty," that is, the state of one ignorant of what is within and outside him (3). Finding "treasure" (see 76 and 109) and "becoming rich" can probably be equated. Logion 110 lets us see that Thomas can commend finding the world even though, possibly to prevent misunderstanding, he shifts to another meaning of the term "world" almost immediately and insists that one must deny the world.

In Logion 80 both meanings of the term world are employed. "He who has known the world has found the body" is a positive statement urging knowledge upon people, "but he who has found the body, the world is not worthy of him," employs "world" as a term of negative comparison meaning, probably, something like "worldly society." By looking at both 110 and 80 it is possible to see that knowing the world is equivalent to finding the world and that becoming rich is equivalent to finding the body. In what way, then, are body and riches similar? If we look to the Wisdom tradition it is obvious that treasure and riches are the reward or consequence of, or even synonymous with, finding Wisdom. Judging by Philo's speculations and the use of "body" imagery in Colossians, the world could be regarded as the "body" of Wisdom (seen by Christians as a body over which Christ is set as head). Thomas may regard the world within which Wisdom is omnipresent as a place containing hidden treasure and as a place which is the body of Wisdom.

Logion 80 is very similar to 56, "He who has known the world has found a corpse, and he who has found a corpse, the world is not worthy of him." The alteration of *soma*, body, to *ptoma*, corpse, or vice versa, is not uncommon in ancient texts (cf. Luke 17:36 *soma*; Matt. 24:28 *ptoma*). Clearly, either "body" has become "corpse" in the transmission of the text of Thomas, or "corpse" has become "body." Though, as we have seen, attempts to credit second and third century gnostics with the creation of Thomas cannot be considered successful, the document did circulate among such groups and did surface in a Nag Hammadi codex. Since such groups were undoubtedly alienated from the physical body, it is more probable that "body" was altered to "corpse" in Logion 56 than vice versa. In any event, since Thomas views favorably the created world, and the Kingdom and light therein, he holds a similarly positive point of view either towards something termed the "body" or something termed the "corpse," and the former seems much more likely. In Logion 60 disciples are told to seek rest "lest you become a corpse." Since rest and immortality are related concepts, "corpse" in 60 is the state of being dead. This is not very subtle or complex. The "corpse" in 60 is something one may, or may not, become; it is *not* what one is from birth. The use of the term body in Logion 80 is enigmatic, but it may imply that the original image to be restored or found is, like the Kingdom and the light, both within and outside mankind.

Thomas does have other logia which speak about the body, and they are ambiguous indeed. They seem to have few theological implications; one may possibly find in them a definite point of view toward embodied human existence but it is a difficult job. Logion 112 says:

> Woe to the flesh which depends on the soul;
> woe to the soul which depends on the flesh.

Here, to all appearances, the flesh is said to suffer under the same heavy burden of depending on the soul as the soul does in depending on the flesh. Nothing could be more ambiguous. The scholars seeking to create a gnostic Thomas find this logion to imply denigration of the flesh. Insofar as it does so, it equally implies a denigration of the soul. Logion 29 seems to say something quite different.

> If the flesh exists because of spirit, it is a miracle, but if spirit (exists) because of the body, it is a miracle of miracles. But I marvel at how this great wealth established itself in this poverty.

In this logion we hear that it is a miracle if flesh exists for the sake of the spirit, or in order to embody the spirit. If, on the other hand, spirit exists in order to animate the body, it is even more miraculous. In both cases a rather positive view of flesh and spirit is in evidence. It is miraculous that spirit has flesh; it is even more miraculous that the body has a spirit. To read these as ironic statements condemning sinful flesh is to conclude that Thomas means the opposite of what it says; this is a dubious and dangerous exegetical technique indeed.

Logion 29 concludes, however, with a negative comment about wealth placed in poverty. This may be a later gloss, and it is hard to know what it means, but by referring to other uses of "wealth" and "poverty" in Thomas we gain some insight. Poverty in Logion 3 is the condition of being ignorant of the Kingdom within oneself; wealth, on the other hand, is the (divine) origin of Adam in Logion 85. Treasure, riches and the like are metaphors for the discovery of the light or the Kingdom or wisdom (cf. 76 and 109). Poverty is, therefore, the condition of a failure to "find," and wealth is a metaphor for success in finding. In Thomas the regions of darkness and light are coextensive (24) and the beginning and end are cotemporal (18). Logion 29 seems to fit this pattern in pointing out that wealth and poverty are coexistent.

Though discerning the light is stressed as good, this does not imply an imprisonment of the light; the light is not released, it is simply apprehended. The Kingdom is not imprisoned within the world. Similarly, though the spirit within the body or the flesh should be apprehended, this does not mean that the flesh is inherently evil. Thomas is content to call the existence of flesh marvelous.

In Logion 87 we encounter another problem:

> The body is wretched which depends on a body,
> and the soul is wretched which depends on these two.

What does it mean to find a soul wretched which depends on a body which depends on a body? This problem can be answered in context. Thomas has a rather odd theme which often goes unnoticed. He is struck by the fact that the process of digestion converts dead meat into living tissue. Logion 60 tells of a Samaritan who, for an utterly obscure reason, has decided to go to Judea to kill and eat a lamb. "As long as it is alive he will not eat it, but (only) if he has killed it and it has become a corpse. . . . You yourselves seek a place for yourselves in rest, lest you become a corpse and be eaten." (Being eaten by worms, vultures, and the like is the unfortunate fate of corpses and not a theological profundity.)

When Logion 7 (the second clause of which seems to have been altered by a careless copyist—cf. Appendix II) states that "Blessed is the lion which the man shall eat, and the lion will become man; and cursed is the man whom the lion shall eat, and the lion will become man," the same theme of digestion appears. If a lion is eaten it is converted into the man that does the eating. We have no evidence within Thomas for any symbolic meaning of the word "lion," if indeed it symbolizes something other than carnivorous behavior. One might postulate "lion" to mean anything from the lion of Judah to the cat-headed/lion-headed Yahve/Jaldabaoth of the Hypostasis of the Archons, but this will lead one in many directions and nowhere. We do not know what "lion" means here save as an example of a carnivore.

Logion 11 stands in the same stream of images:

> This heaven will pass away and your heaven above it will pass away, and the dead do not live, and the living will not die. In the days when you ate the dead, you made it alive; [when you come into the light what will you do?] On the day when

you were one, you became two. But when you have become
two, what will you do?

To begin with, the word "dead" is used here to describe those
who do not find the "life" offered as Thomas' goal. This is similar, if not identical, to the use of the term in such logia as "let
the dead bury their dead" found in another primitive Christian
tradition. Logion 11 seems to contain a pair of parallel questions, but the appearance is deceptive. The second clause of the
first question, "when you come into the light what will you do?"
alludes to a circumstance of positive value, while the second
clause of the second question, "but when you have become two,
what will you do?" refers to a circumstance of negative value;
Thomas insists on the necessity of two becoming one (see 22).

I have placed the second clause of the first question in brack-
ets because there may be a more original version of this saying
in Hippolytus, *Refutatio* V, 8.32. At least Hippolytus' version
preserves a parallelism lost in Thomas' version:

You who have eaten of dead things and have brought them to
life, what will you do if you eat living things?

Quite probably the answer was so obvious to a scribe who copied
Thomas that he gave the answer as the question: "What will you
do if you eat living things?" Why, "you will come into the light!"
Thomas gives a hint of what it means to speak of "eating living
things" in Logion 111, which is a variant of Logion 11:

11   This heaven will pass away and your heaven above it
     will pass away.

111 The heavens and the earth will roll back in your pres-
     ence.

11   The dead do not live, and the living will not die. In the
     days when you ate the dead, you made it alive; when
     you come into the light, what will you do?

111 He who lives by the Living One will not see death.

Logion 11 seems to speak more definitely than the rest of
Thomas about a future end of the world. It is however signifi-

cant that the version in 111 speaks of this event as a possible reality in the present.

Thomas 111 gives the answer to the question implied in Thomas 11 and given in the Hippolytus variant. The full sequence may have been this:

> *In the days when you ate the dead you made it alive.*
> *What will you do if you eat living things?*
> *He who lives by the Living One will not see death.*

Living by the Living One and coming into the light may have been equivalent expressions.

Thomas seems to hold that the standard condition of human life entails the eating of living creatures, which have been made dead, in order to render them living within oneself. This is nothing more than obvious biological fact. He finds this significant and contrasts it with other possibilities, i.e., coming into the light, eating living things or, perhaps, living by means of the Living One. The parallel set of ideas may be this:

1a Ordinarily people eat corpses in order to live.
1b People who fail to find rest will be corpses and themselves be eaten.
2a It would be better to live on the living one/eat living things/come into the light.
2b One would then find rest and immortality.

This whole trend of imagery is rather poorly developed in Thomas; it suffers from textual difficulties in Logion 7 (where the lion becomes man under all circumstances) and in Logion 11 which may have lost an original parallel structure. Nevertheless, it does give us an answer to the question of what it means for a body to depend on a body and the soul to depend on them both (87). The body which depends on a body is the human body which depends for sustenance on the devouring of corpses. Since in 11 "eating the dead" has negative value, presumably a body depending on a body has similar negative value. These expressions derive from Thomas' peculiar symbolism of eating, the positive side of which was eating living things and living on the Living One. This may have had eucharistic significance. To

reify this symbolic system into actual hatred of the human body
would be an error not unlike the error persons of the second
century made in presuming that Christians indulged in literal
cannibalistic feasting.

Thomas' view of the relationship of body and soul and spirit
is unclear. Apparently, as in Philo, Paul, and many others, the
soul and the spirit are given higher valuation than the body.
But such statements as 112, "Woe to the flesh which depends
on the soul; woe to the soul which depends on the flesh," and
29 "If the flesh exists because of spirit, it is a miracle," do not
show any serious or sustained denigration of the physical human
body. After all, if 112 denigrates the body it equally denigrates
the soul. If Thomas is intent upon denigrating both body and
soul in favor of spirit it is very curious that he mentions the
human spirit so infrequently and that it is clearly superior to
soul only in the last line of 29.

Frankly, it would be nice if these matters were more easily
comprehensible. Some authorities are quite confident that
Thomas despises the human body, but their evidence is mainly
derived from texts other than Thomas and from a rather casual
reading of the primary text. In any event, Thomas in 28 claims
that Jesus as Wisdom said, "I stood in the midst of the world,
and I appeared to them in the flesh (*sarx*)," and this shows that
the flesh as the embodiment of Jesus/Wisdom is something as
acceptable to Thomas as it is to John (cf. John 1:14).

Many philosophers in the ancient world had difficulty with
the soul/body/spirit combination. The author of the Wisdom of
Solomon writes that "a perishable body weighs down the soul,
and this tent of clay encumbers a mind full of cares" (9:15).
Philo held a negative view of the human body, as did Paul (cf.
II Cor. 5:6, I Cor. 15:50). If Thomas shares this point of view,
he seems not to make very much of it. What he does make of it
is difficult to discern because of his symbolic use of carnivorous
behavior. *At most* one might conclude that Thomas holds a position somewhat favorable to soul and spirit and somewhat unfavorable to the flesh.

In a general way, Thomas' views can be summarized by saying that he creates a synthesis of Jewish Hellenistic Wisdom and

Jewish apocalyptic thought, merging the tendencies of these two movements into a theory of realized eschatology. Of man Thomas says that he now lives as a "likeness" of God unaware of the light/Kingdom within himself and within the world. Man is a soul and spirit living in flesh, in Thomas' opinion, but nothing very much is made of this fact. Man lives in a world of buying and selling, of family duties and responsibilities. These social values are rejected by Thomas, in logia which are often paralleled in the synoptic gospels (cf. 16, 55, 99, etc.), in favor of a more general love (cf. 25). Social values are rejected by Thomas and are termed "world" as are the people who value them too highly. Wisdom, the mother, should replace one's human mother in one's affections (cf. Logia 101, 105) unless we should understand 105 in light of disparaging Talmudic comments regarding Jesus' legitimacy.

The Gospel of Thomas is primarily concerned with the Wisdom of God, but it never uses the term *sophia*. This could possibly be because Thomas was aware of, and disapproved, extravagant "gnostic" sophia speculations. Still, sophiological conceptions are present throughout Thomas. The world created by God contains light, or is composed of images which contain light, or contains the Kingdom and this is also true of mankind. Discovery of this light or Kingdom is made through the discovery of one's own nature and the discovery of the nature of all creation. This discovery collapses time into a unity; the present is both beginning and end. In the present, which is also the paradisal beginning, man can replace his image or likeness with the image of God possessed by Adam. Man should thus find his light illuminating the world and find the Kingdom in it as well.

Thomas is concerned that persons "find" the Kingdom and the light. This involves looking within, looking outside, returning to the beginning, standing at the end, self knowledge, eschatological revelation, discovery of wisdom, correct apprehension of the world, and so forth. Thomas' language is a rich language and well mixed. It is not systematic, and attempts to make it systematic will never be successful.

Technically, it is impossible to summarize the ideas of the Gospel of Thomas because we do not have any overriding category into which to put his expressions. It would be incorrect to state that what Thomas is really talking about is the Kingdom and so all Wisdom/light imagery should be understood as Kingdom language. Similarly, it would be incorrect to read Thomas as simply stating the views of late Hellenistic Jewish Wisdom with the use of some terminology from the apocalyptic tradition. Thomas does not represent Wisdom or apocalyptic but a synthesis of the two, although Wisdom ideas are unquestionably predominant.

It is better to present Thomas' ideas in schematic form than to try and write a few sentences purporting to summarize them. It is essential to keep in mind that Thomas is capable of mixing, almost at will, the following forms of expression:

1. *Apocalyptic language: Cosmological*
    a. Beginning: Paradise is the Kingdom of God.
    b. Present: Kingdom is upon earth but unseen. Kingdom thought to be above. Mystery of end-time hidden.
    c. End: Return to Paradise/Kingdom, the Kingdom above made below. Mysteries of end-time revealed.

2. *Apocalyptic language: Anthropological*
    a. Beginning: Adam as the androgynous Image of God.
    b. Present: Man is embodied likeness of God only, divided into sexual identities. Man living in social world.
    c. Future: Image of God regained. Kingdom known to be upon the earth. Return to Adamic paradisal state. Replacement of likeness-body with Image-body. Repudiation of social world and its replacement with love of one's brother.

3. *Light/Wisdom language: Cosmological*
    a. Beginning: Light/Wisdom active in creation, source of all things.
    b. Present: Light/Wisdom present in all things or "images" in the world. Wisdom hidden from man and lives above.
    c. Future: World shines with primordial light. Wisdom revealed to man. Arrival of Wisdom as her own last emissary.

4. *Light/Wisdom language: Anthropological*
   a. Beginning: Man comes from light.
   b. Present: Light in man is hidden by darkness, man is empty and in poverty. People seek but do not find, Man is ignorant of self and world.
   c. Future: Man finds light in self and world. Finds treasure/riches and attains rest and reigns.

CHAPTER FIVE

Christology
and Sophiology

I f Christian is a term denoting persons who use the title Christ of Jesus, then Thomas is not a Christian document at all. The word Christ is never used, and so, strictly speaking, Thomas has no *Christ*ology. This is puzzling, for the Jewish Christians of the Pseudo-Clementines, the encratites of the Apocryphal Acts of the Apostles, and virtually all the authors in the Nag Hammadi collection of "gnostic" texts use the term Christ quite freely. Such terms as Savior, Lord, Logos, and Messiah are also missing in Thomas, though they appear in writings from most later Christian circles both orthodox and "heretical." Even the term Son of Man appears but once in Thomas (86) and there means simply "I" or "man" as opposed to animals. The Gospel of Thomas is Christian in a general sense, of course, for the sayings in Thomas are attributed to Jesus.

Is there a tendentious reason for Thomas to have avoided the Christological designations of Jesus ubiquitous in other texts? I cannot imagine what such a reason would have been. Why then does Thomas lack such terminology? Perhaps Thomas was written in a time when such words as Christ, Son of Man, Savior, etc., were not yet universally used of Jesus.

Since Thomas attributes the sayings in his document to Jesus, we will be able by analyzing those sayings to discern a pattern of thought about Jesus. This pattern of thought will constitute the Christology (more precisely, Jesusology) of Thomas.

In the Gospel of Thomas, Jesus speaks as a wise man does, in the form of sayings of the wise, but he is not simply a wise man; he sometimes speaks as Wisdom herself. An intimate of God, agent in creation, revealer of mysteries, the light within which the Image of God is hidden—all these are characteristics of Jesus as Wisdom in the Gospel of Thomas. In sum, the Christology (Jesusology) of the Gospel of Thomas is a naive but thoroughgoing Sophiology.

In Thomas Jesus occupies a category qualitatively distinct from all the messengers of God who preceded him. In reference to the twenty-four books, some accepted as authoritative in Judaism, and probably also in reference to attempts made in the primitive church to discover prophetic proof-texts, his disciples say to him (Logion 52) "Twenty-four prophets spoke in Israel and all of them spoke about you." Jesus replies, "You have left the Living One who is before you and you have spoken about the dead." The term Living One also appears in Logion 59, "Look upon the Living One as long as you live, lest you die and seek to see him and you cannot see," and in Logion 111a, "The heavens and the earth will roll back in your presence, and he who lives by the Living One will not see death." These three logia are the only ones to use the term "Living One." We are urged to remain with, to look upon and, finally, to live by the "Living One." Those who fail to do this will "speak about the dead," "die and fail to see him," and "taste death." The Living One is one who has life at his disposal; the alternative is death.

Who is this "Living One"? In the context of the Gospel of Thomas, as it stands, the Living One is Jesus. The prologue leaves little room for doubt, for it refers to "the secret words which the living Jesus spoke," but the prologue is only debatably part of the original text of Thomas (cf. Appendix I). The statement made in Logion 52—"all of them spoke about you"—is directed to Jesus, and Jesus' response clearly implies that they should look at the Living One (himself) rather than to prophetic texts. Curiously, however, it *may* be implied in Thomas (and I am not certain of this) that inquiry into the nature of Jesus is improper, an erroneous approach to the search for Wisdom.

Thomas contains a variety of logia which are in the form of questions and answers, questions by the disciples as a group

and answers by Jesus. The questions predominantly are about
the time of the end or about the nature of Jesus. In both cases
the disciples' questions seem to indicate their failure to understand.

Questions regarding the end:

18 "Tell us in which way our end will occur."

51 "When will be the rest of the dead and when will the
new world come?"

113 "On what day will the Kingdom come?"

In all three cases the response given by Jesus is that what they
look for is already present, their error is in awaiting it rather
than seeking to discover it.

Questions regarding the nature of Jesus:

24 "Show us the place where you are, for it is necessary for
us to seek it."

37 "On what day will you be revealed to us and on what day
will we see you?"

43 "Who are you that you say these things to us?"

52 "Twenty-four prophets spoke in Israel and all of them
spoke about you."

91 "Tell us who you are so that we can believe in you."

The responses to these questions (or statements requiring response) are similar to those regarding the end time. The answers, Jesus seems to say, are present immediately to the ques-
tioner.

To 24 the response is given that a person should seek the
light within, the same light which lights the whole world. To 37
the answer is instruction for a ritual process (considered in detail in Chapter VII). To 43 the answer is that the nature of Jesus
is to be discerned in the meaning of his sayings, not in his person. To 91 the response is that the disciples do not know how
to examine the present time nor have they known him who is
right in front of them. Finally, 52 receives the response "You
have left the Living One who is before you. . . ." It does *not*

seem to be the case here that a simple identification of Jesus =
Living One is all that is intended. In fact, judging from the
other similar questions and the ambiguous responses they receive, the attempt to determine the nature of Jesus misses the
point that Jesus shares a nature with the light within and
throughout the world (24) and with the essence of the present
time (91), and that his nature is implicit in his sayings (43). In
these questions, and those relating to the time of the end, the
error of the disciples seems to be their search for specific knowledge of a specific person or for a specific date. What counts, the
answers seem to imply, is discovery of the nature of the present
reality, the time or place or person right in front of you.

No doubt, for the Gospel of Thomas Jesus is the Living One.
However, what, or who is the Living One such that the identification of Jesus as Living One is equivalent to the identification of
Jesus with light and with the essential present? The Living One,
the light, the essential existence of Kingdom in the present
are modes of Wisdom.

Wisdom in Jewish literature has life at her disposal: in Proverbs "Long life is in her right hand; in her left hand are riches
and honor" (3:16); words of wisdom "are life to him who finds
them, and healing to all his flesh" (4:22); "The fear of the Lord
is the beginning of wisdom, and the knowledge of the Holy One
is insight. For by me your days will be multiplied, and years
will be added to your life" (9:11). "Whoever finds me finds life,"
says Wisdom in Prov. 8:35. The Wisdom of Solomon tells us
that "in kinship with wisdom there is immortality" (8:17), and
Ben Sirach states that "Wisdom exalts her sons and gives help
to those who seek her. Whoever loves her loves life" (4:11).
Baruch sums up Wisdom's relationship to life and to light: "Learn
where there is wisdom, where there is strength, where there is
understanding, that you may at the same time discern where
there is length of days, and life, where there is light for the
eyes, and peace" (3:14). Jesus, in Thomas, is Wisdom as the
locus and dispenser of life; as such he is the Living One. It may
be implied in Thomas that questions regarding Jesus as an individual are as inappropriate to the search for Wisdom as are

questions about the Kingdom as an event to occur at a future date.

Thomas also refers to God as "living," and his three references all occur in similar contexts. In Logion 50 those who can claim to come from the light can claim to be "his sons and we are the chosen of the living Father." In Logion 3 those who have found the Kingdom within and outside themselves, who know themselves and are known by God are told: "You will know that you are sons of the living Father." Finally, in 37, Jesus is asked by his disciples, "On what day will you be revealed to us and on what day will we see you?" He replies, "When you undress without being ashamed, and you take your clothes and put them under your feet as little children and tramp on them, then you will see the Son of the Living (One) and you will not fear." The question clearly implies that this "Son of the Living" is Jesus himself. But, on the other hand, use of the term "sons of the living Father" for those Christians who have gone through the process outlined in Logia 50 and 3 may mean that they will see themselves to be the sons of the Living. This would let Logion 37 be consistent with 3 and 50.

Thomas seems to use "Living One" as a title for Jesus as Wisdom and "Sons (or chosen) of the living Father" to denote those who have achieved the goals set forth by Thomas and whom we shall henceforth call Christians (with the same reservations as in our use of the term Christology). Jesus himself is never unambiguously called a "Son of the living Father," but it would not be inconsistent for Thomas to have called him this. Jesus refers to God as "my Father" in Thomas 61 and 99. Insofar as Christians have obtained life from the Living One, it seems that they can presume to call themselves Sons of the living Father.

Logion 61 begins with a dichotomy: "Two will be resting on a couch; the one will die, the one will live," and this may mean nothing more than that some persons will find life and some will not. More likely, Thomas believes that one's success in finding life does not depend upon one's own environment and associates and this logion expresses that belief. The remainder of 61 is a dialogue between Salome and Jesus:

> Salome said, "Who are you, man? As if from the One (?) you
> sat on my couch and you ate from my table."
>
> Jesus said to her, "I am He Who Is, from Him Who is the
> same [or undivided]. The things from my Father have been
> given to me."
>
> (Salome said,) "I am your disciple."
>
> (Jesus said to her,) "Therefore, I say, if anyone should be the
> same (lit., deserted) he will be filled with light, but if he is
> divided, he will be filled with darkness.

This is both complex and difficult to translate. The Coptic is rife
with obscurities. Jesus is from the same, a term which should
be taken as a title of the Father. Thomas' Gospel is consistent
in its positive value on unity and on reunion (cf. 22) and in its
scorn of the idea that Jesus came to divide (cf. 72). In Thomas
of course the idea of unity does not apply to the social world
any more than in the synoptic Gospels (cf. 16). Unity is a tran-
scendental and not a mundane ideal. He proceeds to liken his
origin (the same or the undivided) to a goal of Thomasine Christians, that persons should be undivided. Being undivided is here
the equivalent of being filled with light. Being divided is the
equivalent of being filled with darkness. One may be divided or
not, be in the light or not be in the light.

The "things from my Father" which have been given to Jesus
are not specified in this logion. It would not be going too far,
however, to presume that they are life (as discussed above) and
light (cf. 77) and the capacity to bring about union. Jesus is
present when light and life and union are present. Logion 24
reads:

> His disciples said, "Show us the place where you are, for it is
> necessary for us to seek it." He said to them, "He who has
> ears to hear, let him hear. There is light within a man of light
> and he (or, it) lights the whole world. When he (or, it) does
> not shine, there is darkness."

The logion undoubtedly stood alone at an earlier stage of the
transmission of traditions. In Thomas, however, it identifies Jesus' place as the place of light. Jesus dwells in those who have

light and is the light of the world. The disciples can be the light of the world, but not until they seek and find Jesus. This derives from the Wisdom tradition and is Wisdom Christology and is directly related to the *ego eimi* statement of Logion 77:

> I am the light which is above [all things], I am [all things]; [all things] came forth from me and [all things] reached me. Split wood, I am there; lift the stone up, you will find me there."

Jesus is not a messenger or friend of Wisdom here, he is Wisdom itself, creating, illuminating, permeating all things. In reference to human existence, Jesus is Wisdom, the light within those who have light (and even, apparently, the unshining light within those who remain in darkness). Jesus, as Wisdom, comes from the Undivided Father with certain things given to him; he is not God in and of himself.

Philo claimed that the universe came into existence through Wisdom. Wisdom was regarded in Prov. 8:22–31 as the prime agent of God in creation.

Lohse sees that Christians took this aspect of Wisdom seriously and applied it to Jesus Christ.

> All creation owes its existence to the pre-existent Christ. "All things were made through him and without him was not anything made that was made" (John 1:3). "He is the radiance, the glory of God and the very stamp of his essence, upholding the universe by his word of power" (Heb. 1:3).
> All things have been created in him, that is, through him. The fullness of what "all things" means is depicted more exactly by the addition: everything that is in the heavens and on earth (Col. 1:16). There are no exceptions here, all things visible and invisible are included.[1]

In Thomas Jesus is not only creative, in this sense, but also present within creation.

Jesus' coming has two aspects in Thomas. First, just as Wisdom is said to have appeared on earth and lived among men (in the sense of Torah) in Baruch 3:37, and to be present upon earth, calling upon men to accept instruction, to search for her and find her (cf. Prov. 8:1–21), so does Jesus appear on earth, and call upon men to search and find. According to Thomas, Jesus said, "I stood in the midst of the world, and I appeared to them in the flesh" (28). The appearance of Wisdom in the flesh is nowhere mentioned in Jewish Wisdom material, except insofar as Wisdom is embodied in those who have found it. The appearance of Wisdom in the flesh seems to be a particularly Christian idea. While the imagery in Thomas derives from a tradition in which the hypostasis of Wisdom was an accepted idea, the Jesus of Thomas is not a hypostasis but an incarnation.

Jesus' coming in the flesh is implied in every saying in the Gospel of Thomas, insofar as these are sayings attributed to him during a lifetime in which he had disciples, a mother, and opponents, and in which he ate, drank, and responded to questions. Thomas, like the Gospel of John, can be read eisegetically, to imply a Docetic Christology. But Docetic Christians were firm in their beliefs and stated them clearly. No more than John or Q, does Thomas ever make a clearly Docetic statement. Any idea that Thomas is a series of statements by the Risen Christ has no basis in the text. One might find it implied in the term "Living Jesus" of the incipit sentence, but this sentence should be considered apart from the main text, and the term "Living Jesus" can more easily be construed to mean "Jesus when alive," or perhaps "Jesus, giver of life, the Living One." All scholars agree that some of the logia in Thomas are indeed statements made by Jesus when alive.

It was true for all Christians that Jesus' presence did not cease at his death. In one sense the Gospel of Thomas itself is the ongoing presence of Jesus in his words. Thomas is a soteriological residuum of the time of Jesus/Wisdom's appearance in the flesh. The thrust of the Gospel of Thomas is, however, the discovery of the Kingdom and not simply the comprehension of enigmatic phrases.

Jesus' coming has a cosmological aspect. The coming forth of Wisdom occurred prior to creation. This is a central point of the Wisdom poem in Prov. 8:22–31, "The Lord created me at the beginning of his works before all else that he made, long ago. Alone, I was fashioned in times long past, at the beginning, long before earth itself." To find Wisdom one must, in one sense, return to this primordial epoch; "In the place where the beginning is, there the end will be. Blessed is he who will stand at the beginning, and he will know the end and he will not taste death" (18). This conception lies behind the present-eschaton sayings of 11 and 111: "The heavens and the earth will roll back in your presence, and he who lives by the Living One will not see death" (111). The person of whom this can be said is, then, present when only Wisdom and God exist. Jesus/Wisdom's coming forth prior to creation permits the Christian who has found Wisdom, or the Living One, to exist in the present in the beginning. Therefore, in Logion 19 Jesus can say, "Blessed is he who was before he was created." That statement applies equally to Christians and Jesus/Wisdom himself.

The idea of the present force of the creative beginning is present in three consecutive logia, 17, 18, and 19. The first of these is:

> "I will give you what no eye has seen and what no ear has heard and no hand has touched and what has not come into the heart of man."

What Jesus gives that will come into the heart may be Thomas' way of referring to the Spirit of Wisdom attested in the Wisdom of Solomon and elsewhere. In the context of Thomas what is given pertains to the primordial beginning and to the present.

Paul, who quotes a similar saying in 1 Cor. 2:9, refers it to Wisdom in the primordial beginning:

> But we impart a secret and hidden wisdom of God, which God decreed before the ages for our glorification. None of the rulers of this age understood this; for if they had, they would not have crucified the Lord of glory. But, as it is written, "What no eye has seen, nor ear heard, nor the heart of man conceived, what God has prepared for those who love him," God has revealed to us through the Spirit. (1 Cor. 2:7–10)

What is implicit in Thomas is stated clearly by Paul.

Wisdom's capacity to reveal the secret and hidden things of God is frequently attested in Jewish Wisdom literature, as is the idea that this capacity derives from Wisdom's presence at creation. Jesus, as Wisdom, has this role in Thomas. He possesses the secrets, the hidden things, the mysteries of God (cf. 17, 5, 6).

Thomas' themes of the light within all things (77) and of the Kingdom spread out upon the earth (113) imply that one finds Jesus who is the light (77) not only in the person Jesus but also within the world. Thomas reports that the disciples said to Jesus, "Tell us who you are so that we can believe in you." His reply is, "You examine the face of the heavens and the earth, and (yet) you have not known him who is in front of your face, nor do you know how to examine this time" (91). Space, person, and time are combined here. The disciples apprehend none of these correctly.

Thomas' apocalyptic background is evident in the idea of examining the time, for one of the central themes of apocalyptic is that there is a "divine determination of times" (in the words of Von Rad), and that the secret end of mundane time will be revealed at the culmination of history or, for special persons, earlier. To Thomas the culmination of history is present. In Logion 91 Thomas characteristically unites several themes: the Kingdom can be sought in the heavens and the earth, and found by apprehending "him who is in front of your face," and in terms of the present time. The secret things are presently in a state of potential manifestation if they are not perceived correctly; they are in a state of actual manifestation if they are perceived correctly. In Logion 5 Jesus says, "Know what is in front of your face, and what is concealed from you will be revealed to you. For there is nothing concealed which will not be manifest." Here, instead of the personal "him who is in front of your face" given in response to the question "Tell us who you are" in 91, we have the impersonal "what is in front of your face." As light is within all things, so Jesus who is light is within all things (77) and so he is in front of you in the present. This is, ultimately, the self-revelation of Wisdom, of creation, and of Jesus. It is not pantheism; God is not equated with all things. It is what one might call a pan-Sophical assertion that Jesus as Wisdom is in all times and places in creation. To know what is in front of your face, or what is present before you, to examine this time or the one who is in front of you is to know this world, this time, and Jesus/Wisdom simultaneously.

Hengel shows that such sophiological Christology has roots in the very early church:

> Following the well-known saying in the Epistle of Barnabas, "Behold I make the last things as the first things" (6:13), the eschatological awareness of the earliest community was matched by a certain interest in protology. Only the one who has control over the beginning has the whole matter in his grasp. The beginning therefore *had* to be illuminated by the end, and ultimately the *idea of pre-existence* was a favorite means of bringing out the special significance of particular phenomena for salvation. (Hengel's emphasis)
>
> It is typically Jewish that in the exposition of Christology, pre-existence, mediation at creation and the idea of sending the Son into the world were all developed chronologically *before the legends of the miraculous birth of Jesus.* The tradition behind the prologue to the Fourth Gospel is 'earlier' than the infancy narratives of Matthew and Luke in their present form. (Hengel's emphasis)
>
> Once the idea of pre-existence had been introduced, it was obvious that the exalted Son of God would also attract to himself the functions of Jewish Wisdom as a mediator of creation and salvation. Even Wisdom, which was associated with God in a unique way from before time, could no longer be regarded as an independent entity over against the risen and exalted Jesus and superior to him. Rather, all the functions of Wisdom were transferred to Jesus, for "in him are hid all the treasures of wisdom and knowledge" (Col. 2:3).[2]

The presence of Jesus and the disclosure of God's secret are both aspects of the logia in Thomas. It is through apprehension of the meaning of the logia that the Christian finds union, life, light, Jesus/Wisdom, and indeed becomes undivided, living, has light within, and is as Jesus is. These themes lie behind Thomas 13 and 108, which are logia of considerable importance. We read in 13 that,

> Jesus said to his disciples, "Make a comparison and tell who I am like."
>
> Simon Peter said to him, "You are like a righteous angel."

> Matthew said to him, "You are like a wise man."
>
> Thomas said to him, "Master, my mouth will not be able to say what you are like."
>
> Jesus said, "I am not your master because you drank; you are drunk from the bubbling spring which I measured."
>
> And he took him; he went aside. He spoke to him three words (or sayings). When Thomas returned to his companions, they asked him, "What did Jesus say to you?"
>
> Thomas said to them, "If I tell you one of the words (or sayings) which he said to me, you will pick up stones; you will throw them at me. And fire will come from the stones and consume you."

At the beginning three disciples make statements. These are probably in ascending order of accuracy: Jesus is not an angel; Jesus is not one who has found Wisdom; Jesus cannot be compared to any other thing.

The latter portion of saying 13 is very obscure. Punishment by stoning indicates that the three words would be thought blasphemous under Jewish law and, in this instance, even one would be sufficient to bring about such a punishment. The idea of throwing stones that give forth fire is somewhat reminiscent of Logion 10 where Jesus says, "I have thrown fire on the world, and behold, I guard it until it is on fire," and of Logion 16, "Men might think I have come to throw peace on the world, and they do not know that I have come to throw dissolution on the earth; fire, sword, war." "World" in this context is most naturally taken to refer to the social world since war (= sword?) is a social disruption.

World, by extension, also refers to those who fail to comprehend the import of his coming. One might presume therefore that the very stones they throw will cast fire upon the throwers who fail to comprehend what was given to Thomas. Not much more than this can be said about this latter portion of Logion 13. It is easy to make clever guesses about the identity of the three mysterious words, or logia, but it will be best to refrain from such guesswork. Thomas has been given "what no ear has heard" (17), but we have not.

We can understand a good bit more about the initial dialogue between Thomas and Jesus in 13 because the ideas contained in it are also contained in Logion 108. In this logion Jesus says, "He who drinks from my mouth will be as I am, and I will be he, and the things that are hidden will be revealed to him." Thomas, in 13, having "become drunk from the bubbling spring which I (Jesus) measured," is one who has become drunk from Jesus' mouth and become as he is. Thomas does not become Jesus, he becomes as Jesus is, which, since Jesus is light, life, union, etc., means that Thomas "shines" light forth, finds life, achieves union—all themes which have been discussed previously. The idea of drinking from Jesus' mouth is the same as the idea of becoming drunk from the bubbling spring which Jesus measured.

The idea that the words of Wisdom are a fountain is present in the older Wisdom tradition. In a passage of Baruch (3:10–14) this image introduces a series of sentences containing terms also important to Thomas. There the fountain of Wisdom is the source of life, light, and peace.

Ben Sirach says that the law "will feed him with the bread of understanding, and give him the water of wisdom to drink" (15:3). Further, in 24:21 we find the following passage wherein Wisdom praises herself: "Those who eat me will hunger for more, and those who drink me will thirst for more." To drink from the mouth of Jesus is to drink from the mouth of Wisdom.

Jesus, as Wisdom, communicates through wise sayings and parables as does the wise man accordint to Ben Sirach 39:6: "If it is the will of the great Lord he will be filled with a spirit of intelligence; then he will pour forth wise sayings of his own. . . ." On the other hand, one seeking Wisdom "preserves the sayings of famous men and penetrates the intricacies of parables. He investigates the hidden meaning of proverbs and knows his way among riddles" (39:2–3). It is hard to imagine a more apt description of one who seeks to "interpret the meaning of these sayings," in Thomas.

In Logion 13 Thomas is established as a prototype of the one who utilizes the Gospel of Thomas. To drink from the fountain, or drink from Jesus' mouth, is equivalent to drinking from Wisdom, and this is done by means of investigating and penetrating the intricacies of parables and proverbs (cf. Prologue and Logion 1). He who does this becomes as Jesus is and, implicitly (in accordance with Ben Sirach 39:6), he will be capable of pouring forth wise sayings of his own through a spirit of Wisdom. We hear in 108 that he will have revealed to him the things that are hidden.

It is not correct to say that Jesus in Thomas is filled with such a spirit of Wisdom; he *is* Wisdom. But it may be correct to presume that such a spirit fills one who becomes as Jesus is. This would mean that becoming as Jesus is gives one the key to hidden things and the capacity of speaking those things. In 13 Thomas evidently has such a capacity but refrains from making use of it. Perhaps the statement "I will be he" in Logion 108 implies that the spirit of Jesus (which in Thomas cannot be considered distinct from the spirit of Wisdom) will enter that person.

Logion 92 has Jesus make a very odd statement:

> Search and you will find, but those things which you asked me in those days, I did not tell you then; now I want to speak them, and you do not ask about them.

If we take this in the context of the Gospel of Thomas, it means that the sayings in Thomas itself are in some fashion inadequate. They are, after all, things which disciples did ask about in days past and things about which Jesus did tell them. There is, implicitly, more to be said by Jesus and the difficulty is that people do not ask. If one becomes as Jesus, one can ask new questions and provide new answers, generate sayings, utter things Jesus now wishes to speak. It is common knowledge that the New Testament contains numerous sayings supposedly spoken by Jesus after his death, and such spirit-inspired sayings may well also make up portions of the Gospel of Thomas.

When Thomas says in Logion 29 that if the spirit exists for the sake of the body it is "a miracle of miracles," and then goes on to "marvel at how this great wealth established itself in this poverty," it may be that the spirit in question is not the human spirit at all but the spirit of Wisdom/Jesus. In this case the wealth that comes into poverty may be the arrival of the spirit, correlative with the "finding" of the treasure. It is quite difficult to tell when Thomas speaks anthropologically and when he speaks soteriologically. The likelihood is that these categories are ours and not his at all. In any event, Thomas is perfectly capable of using the same term in two different senses, as we have already seen, and he may refer to the embodied human spirit as miraculous, and the spirit of Wisdom/Jesus in the body as even more miraculous, in the same saying.

As Logion 92 speaks of searching and finding and of people who at present do not ask Jesus things which were left unsaid in earlier days, so Logion 38 says,

> Many times you desired to hear these words which I say to you and you have no one else from whom to hear them. There will be days when you will seek me, and you will not find me.

Obviously Jesus is the one from whom one may or may not hear the words, and the question is whether the logia of Thomas exhaust the possibility of hearing his words or whether one can persist in hearing them in the present through the spirit of Wisdom/Jesus. We can turn to Prov. 2:23–28—the source for Logion 38—for a possible answer.

> When they call upon me, I will not answer them;
> When they search for me, they shall not find me. (Prov. 2:28).

If we suppose that Thomas does not speak of the impossibility of finding Jesus (and he clearly does not do so in the other logia), what hope does he hold out? Prov. 2:23 provides an answer: "If only you would respond to my (Wisdom's) reproof, I would give you my spirit and teach you my precepts." Thomas may be saying in 38 that you will have no one *else* if you do not have Jesus, but that the possibility of having Jesus is open to those who seek and find correctly. There seems to be implicit in Thomas the idea that by comprehending the logia available in the text one gains the possibility of hearing further words from Wisdom/Jesus through the spirit.

It would be surprising indeed if Jesus as Wisdom were not to give to Christians what Wisdom herself is commonly said to give her adherents: the spirit of Wisdom and the consequent capacity to generate *logoi sophon*. While this is not ever stated clearly in Thomas, it does seem that Christians may expect this benefit. This is probably what is meant by "He . . . will be as I am, and I will be he," in Logion 108.

Jesus is fully identified with Wisdom incarnate in Logion 28. This logion has its roots in Prov. 2:20–33 and related sources, which tell of the rejection of Wisdom by fools. Logion 28 seems to have two parts, one interpolated within the other. Jesus says,

> a. I stood in the midst of the world, and I appeared to them in the flesh. I found all of them drunk; I did not find any of them thirsting.
>
> b. And my soul was pained for the sons of men because they are blind in their heart, and they do not see that they came empty into the world; they seek to go out of the world empty.
>
> However, they are drunk.
>
> a. When they have shaken off their wine, then they shall repent.

In this sequence Jesus/Wisdom uses the term drunk in contrast with the term thirsting. In light of Logion 13 we can see that the contrast is less between drunkenness and sobriety than between the sources from which one may drink. Jesus comes in the flesh to present people the option of drinking from his mouth, as in 13 and 108. Those who do not so drink are described, in the interpolation, as "empty." This condition is rectified by means of being undivided and hence "filled" with light, as Thomas states in the conclusion of Logion 61:

> If anyone should be the same (undivided) he will be filled with light, but if he is divided, he will be filled with darkness.

Darkness and emptiness are, apparently, interchangeable terms, depending on the metaphoric system being employed.

The idea that Jesus came in the flesh is here correlated with the idea of thirsting; the idea that Jesus is the light which is within the world, through which the world came into being, is correlated with the idea of people being filled either with light or darkness. The coming in the flesh, the coming of the fountain, the coming forth of light are various metaphorical schemes, they are not separate Christologies. Jesus is identified with Wisdom, and Wisdom was conceived in ancient Judaism in a multiplicity of ways. Consequently Jesus is, in Thomas, conceived in a multiplicity of ways, and those ways are the ways of Wisdom.

Martin Hengel writes:

> The remarkable number of names applied to Wisdom and the various ways of conceiving of it, and even more the similar variety in the case of Philo's Logos, show us that it is misleading to unravel the web of christological titles into a number of independent and indeed conflicting "christologies," with different communities standing behind each. . . . Ancient man did not think analytically or make differentiations within the realm of myth in the way we do, but combined and accumulated his ideas in a "multiplicity of approximations."[3]

Hengel is not thinking of the Gospel of Thomas, but his observations are apt. The multiplicity of terms for Jesus that we find in Thomas focus on, or coalesce around, Wisdom, but no one is correct. Thomas has a naive sophiological Christology based upon a simple attribution to Jesus of what was said and thought of Wisdom in Jewish texts. Thomas recognizes the historical reality of Jesus, credits him with flesh, a mother, disciples and, above all else, sayings spoken during his life, but the events of Jesus' life and death are not important to him. Thomas may also maintain that Christians can and should receive the spirit of Wisdom/Jesus and thus generate sayings concerning matters of which Jesus did not speak in his own time. This, however, is a consequence of "finding" and not itself the central goal; it therefore receives little stress.

The same caution Hengel urges in Christology must be applied in soteriology as well. It is a trait of some contemporary scholars that they choose, out of a welter of soteriological indications, one which they prefer or one which they wish to decry. In the ancient world soteriological possibilities were not so neatly categorized as they now seem to be. Thomas, for instance, finds salvation inherent in discovering the Kingdom spread upon the earth (113), *and* in making an image in place of an image (22), *and* in apprehending what is in front of one's face (5), *and* in loving one's brother as one's soul (25), *and* in seeking and finding the treasure of Wisdom, etc. Thomas does not represent this or that discrete soteriological system; rather, as a man of the ancient world, he is content with a "multiplicity of approximations."

For Thomas, Jesus is light, life, union, and he may be spirit as well. Some of the things of his Father have been given to him. He is from the light, from the Undivided, he is the Living One. Jesus is the beginning and the end; where he is the light is and the Kingdom is. Thus, to find the Kingdom in the world is to find the light, and to find the concealed secret of God is to find Jesus.

Jesus is one who presents his word as something salvific. He requires hearing, interpreting, choice, and decision in the present. No one is inherently saved or damned in Thomas. One who drinks from Jesus' mouth can become as he is and have Jesus say, "I am he." The same Kingdom is spread upon the earth for everyone.

Thomas does not have a Christology which is systematic and analytical. His Christology is a synthesis; it works with images and not with univocal definitions. In fact, Thomas' Christology, though multifold, is less complicated than it seems. If one begins with the proposition that Jesus is Wisdom, and then turns to Jewish Wisdom literature and to some Wisdom-influenced Apocalyptic literature (e.g., that of Qumran) for specifications of Wisdom, Thomas' Christology will come forth in full multiplicity and carry with it an equal multiplicity of soteriological metaphors.

It is difficult to pronounce upon the antiquity of this synthesis. It may go back to Jesus himself; certainly it can be traced to the middle decades of the first century. In Hengel's opinion,

> the connection between Jesus and Wisdom had . . . been prepared for by Jesus' own preaching during his ministry, the form of which was very much in the wisdom tradition. The

primitive Palestine community collected the unique wisdom teachings of the Messiah in the nucleus of the logia source, just as the wise sayings of King Solomon, David's son, had also been collected together. Of course, in the case of Jesus, 'more than Solomon is here' (Luke 11.31 = Matt. 12:42). He was seen already as the representative of divine Wisdom, and the features of Wisdom which we also find in the case of the Son of Man in the Jewish Similitudes of Ethiopian Enoch were transferred to him.[4]

We began this chapter with the observation that the Gospel of Thomas has no Christology, properly so-called, because it lacks the term Christ, as well as such terminology as Son of Man, messiah, savior, Son of God, etc. It is not impossible that Thomas derives from a time when such terms were not yet in common use in reference to Jesus.

CHAPTER SIX

Thomas and the New Testament

For many decades scholars have assumed that the simpler the Christology, the more primitive and hence the earlier it is. This assumption falls apart when we realize that the complex Christology of Paul is, and remains, the earliest of which we have any written and reliably datable record. The complexity of a Christology is no criterion for its date. If it were so, we would have to date Acts several decades, if not several generations, earlier than Paul, whose history Acts purports to relate.

It is important to realize that Christologies in the New Testament period, as in subsequent periods, do not arise wholly anew but arise in response to already existing trends and systems of thought. For example, diverse Jewish reflections upon a coming Son of Man were brought over into christological theories. While one Christian might select some characteristics and reject others, the possibility was open for him simply to identify Jesus with the Son of Man and adopt the whole of prior Son of Man speculation christologically.

The same is true for sophiological Christology. To identify Jesus and Wisdom was immediately to identify Jesus with all those aspects of Wisdom which were known to a given Christian—often more aspects than are known to us, for the few documents of Wisdom literature that remain to us in the twentieth century are but a remnant of what in the first century was a literate, creative, and ancient tradition. A Christian leader of a primitive church would not have identified Jesus with Wisdom

and have expected his followers to understand that he intended
but one or two aspects of Wisdom to be considered relevant.

The Johannine sophiological Christology is a case in point.
Therein Jesus is not simply *logos* and nothing else. Jesus is light,
life, dispenser of living water, and so on. On Jesus are placed
manifold sophiological developments of first-century Judaism.
One cannot seek to trace, independently, the Johannine motifs
of *logos,* and then of life, and then of light, and so forth, as
though these concepts were brought together uniquely by John.
These aspects of divine reality were combined into a conceptual
unity decades or centuries earlier. For John to say of Jesus, for
example, that he is the Light of the World implies, through pre-
Johannine Wisdom literature, that Jesus is *therefore* one from
whom comes waters of life, though of course one is free not to
pursue the implication.

Perhaps, by shifting terms, I can make the matter clearer.
Imagine, then, that a Christian were to put forth the thesis that
Jesus is the Buddha. He would not have to invent independently his categories of thought and expression, his views of the
world and of the goals of mankind. He would only have to bring
existing Christian traditions (and we may assume he would
choose those which suited him) into relationship with his choice
of existing Buddhist traditions. His Christology might include
such concepts as sambhogakaya, nirvana, dharma, dukkha,
prajna, the four noble truths, and whatever else he knew and
found significant.

What this means is that a sophiological Christology derived
from identification of Jesus and Wisdom could, and probably
would, have become a complex Christology in a matter of years
and not decades. On the other hand, persons concerned primarily with other possibilities of Christology may simply have
chosen to identify Jesus with Wisdom and let it go at that, directly borrowing relatively little material from the rich and elab-
orated Wisdom tradition. Both Q and Matthew seem to have
done this, and their doing so indicates that the identification of
Jesus and Wisdom was virtually a commonplace in their environments, worthy of acknowledgment rather than of elabora-
tion.

Paul, in First Corinthians, says that Jesus is the Wisdom of God (1:24) for, like his opponents, he identified the two. The letter to Colossians, by a follower of Paul, also contains such an identification, as does the Gospel of John. The author of the letter to the Ephesians writes that

> To me, though I am the very least of all the saints, this grace was given, to preach to the Gentiles the unsearchable riches of Christ, and to make all men see what is the plan of the mystery hidden for ages in God who created all things; that through the church the manifold wisdom of God might now be made known to the principalities and powers in the heavenly places. This was according to the eternal purpose which he has realized in Christ Jesus our Lord. (Eph. 3:8–11)

Here too Jesus and God's Wisdom are identified. In fact, one might well say that in the period ca. A.D. 50–90 the question was not so much whether one identified Jesus and Wisdom but what implications one drew from that identification. Any idea shared by Matthew, Paul, Q, John, the Corinthian opponents of Paul, the authors of Colossians and Ephesians, and, for that matter, the author of the Letter to Hebrews was a common and ancient idea indeed.

Both Q and Matthew, who used Q, identify Jesus with Wisdom. Matthew heightens the identification that he finds in his source Q. Several sayings in Q indicate that this identification has been made; Luke 10:21f. and Matt. 11:25f. is a case in point. The passage reads, in Luke,

> I thank thee, Father, Lord of heaven and earth, that thou hast hidden these things from the wise and understanding and revealed them to babes; yea, Father, for such was thy gracious will. All things have been delivered to me by my Father; and no one knows who the Son is except the Father, or who the Father is except the Son and any one to whom the Son chooses to reveal him.

This is, in the words of Elisabeth Fiorenza, Q's latest stage which "identifies (Jesus) with Wisdom herself insofar as the relationship between son and father is conceived in terms of the relationship between the heavenly Sophia and God."[1] In James Robinson's opinion,

> what is most significant for our purposes is that here, even if at the very latest stage in the Q tradition, Jesus is not simply cast in the role of one of Sophia's spokesmen even the culminating one, but rather is described with predications that are reserved for Sophia herself.[2]

It is not possible, in this space, to argue at length for the antiquity of this pericope of Q, as opposed to its existence in "the very latest stage," but the argument that it is late depends upon the prevailing view that Q represents a very early eschatological Son of Man preaching which supposedly derives in the main from Jesus himself. This view is by no means unanimously shared by scholars. For example, Koester claims that there was an earlier "version of Q in which the apocalyptic expectation of the Son of man was missing, and in which Jesus' radicalized eschatology of the kingdom and his revelation of divine wisdom in his own words were dominant motifs."[3] Indeed, it is an interesting experiment to look at the Q sayings which are neither Wisdom sayings (as determined by Suggs) nor sayings present in Thomas.[4] The remaining sayings have a remarkable consistency: concern with John the Baptist, eschatological parallels drawn in reference to the Old Testament prophetic figures and scenes, struggle with the devil and his minions, and a kind of preaching in the form of "as you do X, so X will be done to you."

At the time of Q the *option* of a highly complex sophiological Christology existed. The author of Q did not take much advantage of this option; Matthew, who used Q, took more advantage of it.

Matthew, however, *assumes* an identity of Jesus and Wisdom, and so writes his gospel. He does not, to all appearances, strongly stress this identity, nor deal with it in a novel or even particularly significant way. That Jesus can speak as Wisdom itself is something Matthew assumes his community will find acceptable. For example, what in Luke is given as a quotation of the Wisdom of God by Jesus is attributed directly to Jesus in Mat-

thew (Luke 11:49; Matt. 23:34). Robinson writes that "in the
last stage of Q . . . the shift to a Sophia Christology has been
made. This Sophia Christology that emerges at the end of the
Q tradition comes to fruition in Matthew, which in general seems
to carry forward the Q trajectory more than does Luke."[5] "It
would not," M.J. Suggs writes, "greatly overstate the case to
say that *for Matthew* Wisdom has 'become flesh and dwelled
among us' (John 1:14)." He believes that "Matthew has consciously modified the saying about 'Wisdom's children' into one
about 'Wisdom's deeds' *in order to identify Jesus with Wisdom.*"
Matthew, he believes,

> proceeds to an identification of Jesus with Sophia. It now be-
> comes apparent that the long-recognized sayings belonging to
> the Wisdom tradition are not merely outcroppings above the
> surface of Matthean Christology. As it had done for Paul and
> subsequently did for John, speculation about the pre-existent
> Sophia constituted an important element in Matthew's under-
> standing of Christ.[6]

This I believe to be true and well demonstrated in Suggs's book.
Matthew makes the identification of Jesus and Wisdom rather
casually, however. In a few pericopes it is obvious; in the Gospel of Matthew as a whole it is present. Matthew assumes his
readers will share this perception with him and finds no need
to belabor the point.

As I Cor. 1:24 and later Pauline texts indicate, one can safely
believe that Paul and his followers identified Wisdom and Jesus.
By the time of Matthew, and the time of the Q with which
Matthew worked, Paul's identification was thirty or so years old.

The identification of Jesus and Wisdom *can* immediately carry
with it the entirety of the Wisdom tradition. It need not do so,
of course. Still, the identification of Jesus and Wisdom needs
neither long evolution, the passage of years, nor the emergence
of theological genius to imply the whole Wisdom tradition.

Toward the beginning of the letter to the Colossians and at
the beginning of the Gospel of John are hymns which have much
in common: Col. 1:15–20 and John 1:1–5, 10–14, 16–18. Käsemann believed that the hymn in Colossians was a pre-Christian

gnostic hymn, and Bultmann believed the same of the hymn in John. More recent scholarship has turned away from this interpretation, and both hymns are now more commonly thought to derive from the Wisdom tradition. Lohse says, of the hymn in Colossians, that "the exalted Christ is called 'the image of God, the first-born of all creation,' and he is also called 'the beginning.' With these designations the hymn relates to the characterizations which Hellenistic synagogues gave to Wisdom."[7] He goes on to point out, in reference to this hymn, that the Hellenistic synagogues found that "Wisdom is not only the mediatrix of creation but also of salvation, and cosmology and soteriology are related to one another in the myth of Wisdom."[8] Similarly, Brown writes of the hymn that begins the Gospel of John, wherein the term *logos* is of primary importance, that

> in the OT presentation of Wisdom, there are good parallels for almost every detail of the Prologue's description of the Word. The Prologue has carried personification further than the OT did in describing Wisdom, but that development stems from the Incarnation. If we ask why the hymn of the Prologue chose to speak of "Word" rather than of "Wisdom," the fact that in Greek the former is masculine while the latter is feminine must be considered. Moreover, the relation of "Word" to the apostolic kerygma is a relevant consideration.[9]

The terminology in these two hymns is by no means absent from the remainder of Colossians and John, and in both the identification of Jesus with Wisdom is more fully developed.

In Colossians and John, especially in the two hymns, certain terms and conceptions appear prominently that are also prominent in Thomas. The beginning and the creative activity of Jesus Christ therein is stressed (John 1:1–3, Col. 1:16–17, Thomas 18, 77). The words "light," "life," "image," are of major importance, as they are in Thomas, and in John it is only in this hymn that we hear that the Word became *sarx* (cf. Thomas 28). Thomas' central themes of the Kingdom and of the revealing of hidden things are present in Colossians just prior to this hymn (1:12) and just after its completion (1:26–27). The Colossians hymn uses the term *"ta panta"* (1:16–17), the All or all things, which occurs also throughout Thomas (e.g., 2, 67, 77). It is probably significant that both the letter of Colossians generally (cf. 2:12, 2:20, 3:10–12) and John in its first chapter especially (1:24–34) have to do with the rite of baptism. We shall see that this rite was of importance to Thomas as well.

Colossians is not Johannine; John is not Pauline; Thomas is neither Pauline nor Johannine in any full sense. The hymns in Colossians and in John were certainly in existence, and probably in liturgical use prior to the writing of either the letter or the gospel. This provides further indication that the identification of Jesus and Wisdom was made early in the first century. It is hard to imagine that any one of these three (John, Thomas, Colossians) is "gnostic" in a way that will permit the other two to be non-gnostic; but none is gnostic. All three are derived from the tendency of primitive Christianity to apply to Jesus terms and concepts of the Wisdom tradition. While John here uses the word *logos* and not *sophia*, Colossians and Thomas use neither *logos* nor *sophia* for Jesus. The latter two probably came from a time before logos-Christology, properly so-called, came into being.

The identification of Wisdom and Jesus is built into and underlies much of the early Christian literature we possess. It is not foreign to Q, Matthew, Paul, John, Colossians, Hebrews or Ephesians. It is the property of no one "gattung" and no one ancient theologian. It can be rather casual (as in Matthew and Q) or of central significance (as in John and Colossians). The identification of Wisdom and Jesus always has the potential of leading immediately to full utilization of Wisdom speculations in reference to Jesus. Those authors who refrain from this do so because they have other points they hold to be more important. Those authors who do not hold back in this regard find the identification of Wisdom and Jesus one of the major points they wish to make.

Thomas and John

Raymond Brown, in his article "The Gospel of Thomas and St. John's Gospel," says, "I wish to emphasize that throughout even when John and GTh use the same terms, they often use them in an entirely different theological framework. *Presuming* GTh is the later work, we find a theological adaptation and re-orientation of gospel [i.e., John] ideas in GTh" (Emphasis added.).[10] Brown acknowledges that he operates on the assumption that Thomas is a gnostic document although he notes objections to this raised by W. C. van Unnik.[11] As I do not believe that Thomas is gnostic, I shall presume that when John and Thomas share christological conceptions and vocabulary derived from Sophiology, the similarities in derivation, conception, and vocabulary indicate a similarity of theological orientation, which is modified but not eliminated by the divergence of the literary forms and particular emphases of the two documents. Thomas' theology is not identical to that of John, but neither is it "entirely" different.

In the next few pages I shall take advantage of Brown's well worked-out set of parallels between the Gospel of John and Wisdom literature (in his Anchor Bible commentary on John) to show that, to a large extent, what he says is true for John and Wisdom literature is also true for Thomas and Wisdom literature. Brown writes that

> Lady Wisdom existed with God from the beginning even before there was an earth (Prov viii 22–23; Sir xxiv 9; Wis vi 22)—so also the Johannine Jesus is the Word who was in the beginning (i 1) and was with the Father before the world existed (xvii 5).[12]

Käsemann, writing on John, finds this theme to be of exceptional significance. He claims that

> John . . . places the community . . . in the situation of the beginning when the Word of God came forth and called the world out of darkness into light and life. This beginning is not a past occurrence in saving history which is lost for ever. It is instead the new reality eschatologically revealed. . . . The community under the Word lives and exists from the place granted to it in the presence of the Creator and from its ever-new experience of the first day of creation in its own life. This is the meaning of the dogmatic Christology in our Gospel.[13]

The sophiological Christology Brown traces within the Wisdom tradition has soteriological implications in the Gospel of John. It does so as well in Thomas. There we find both Logia 18 and 19 referring to the beginning soteriologically, "In the place where the beginning is, there the end will be. Blessed is he who will stand at the beginning, and he will know the end and he will not taste death," and "Blessed is he who was before he was created." These ideas are reflective of a sophiological Christology insofar as Jesus/Wisdom is the one who was before creation, and it may also reflect the experience of such Christians as are united with Jesus. Logion 77, "I am the light which is above all of them, I am all things, all things came forth from me and all things reached me," contains a combination of motifs that all things came into being through Wisdom/Jesus, that Jesus is light and that light was the condition of the initial day of creation. These ideas are not foreign to John.

Brown points out that

> Wisdom is said to be a pure emanation of the glory of the Almighty (Wis vii 25)—so also Jesus has the Father's glory which he makes manifest to men (i 14, viii 50, xi 4, xvii 5, 22, 24). Wisdom is said to be a reflection of the everlasting light of God (Wis vii 26); and in lighting up the path of men (Sir 1 29), she is to be preferred to any natural light (Wis vii 10, 29)—in Johannine thought God is light (I John i 5); and Jesus who comes forth from God is the light of the world and of men (John i 4–5, vii 12, ix 5), ultimately destined to replace all natural light (Rev xxi 23).[14]

Brown finds something of the same complexity in the Johannine idea of light (wherein God is light and Jesus is the light of the world) as one finds in Thomas' conception of light. In Logia 83 and 84, discussed above, a distinction is made between the light and the image of the light. The light of the world may be, in Thomas, the image of the light which is within the manifest images which compose the world. When, in 83, Thomas writes that (God's) image is hidden in (God's) light, he may be making a distinction of the same order as John's. Neither the "light of the world" nor "the image of the light" are the same as the light which is the everlasting light of God.

Certainly in Thomas light which illuminates man's path is to be preferred to any natural light and may replace it (although Thomas does not conceive of this replacement in an eschatological sense). Thomas writes, in 24, "His disciples said, 'Show us the place where you are, for it is necessary for us to seek it.' He said to them, 'He who has ears to hear, let him hear. There is light within a man of light and he (or, it) lights the whole world. When he (or, it) does not shine, there is darkness.' " Jesus is indirectly identified with light in this passage. Moreover, this quotation is in accord with John's pattern of thought. There is a duality between light and darkness; Jesus is found where light is; Jesus who comes from God (cf. 61) is the light of the world and of men.

Returning to Brown:

> Wisdom is described as having descended from heaven to dwell with men (Prov. viii 31; Sir xxiv 8; Bar. iii 37; Wis ix 10; James iii 15)—so also Jesus is the Son of Man who has descended from heaven to earth (i 14, iii 31, vi 38, xvi 28). In particular John iii 13, is very close to Bar iii 29 and Wis ix 16–17. The ultimate return of Wisdom to heaven (En xlii 2) offers a parallel to Jesus' return to his Father.[15]

Thomas is not interested in Jesus' return to his Father in a Johannine sense although that return is clearly implied in Logion 38. He does speak of Jesus' coming from the same (61) and in Logion 28 Jesus speaks as incarnate Sophia, saying "I stood in the midst of the world, and I appeared to them in the flesh." This has similarities both to the idea of Wisdom's descent from heaven and to John's "the Word was made flesh and dwelt among us" (John 1:14).

Thomas, as indicated in Logion 108, stresses the unity of Christians with Jesus, although he does not assert their full identity with Jesus. Käsemann claims that Johannine Christians may hope to experience the first day of creation in their own lives. Thomas contains the same idea in 18, "Blessed is he who will stand at the beginning," which introduces the ambiguity of 19, "Blessed is he who was before he was created." As the existence in the present of the condition of the beginning is taken quite seriously by John, so it is by Thomas. One who is now in the beginning is now before he was created. Statements in Thomas that Christians "come from the light" (50) and that they come from the Kingdom and will return there again (49), are true in Thomas because they are true of Jesus.

In Brown's judgment,

> the function of Wisdom among men is to teach them of the things that are above (Job xi 6–7; Wis ix 16–18), to utter truth (Prov viii 7; Wis vi 22), to give instructions as to what pleases God and how to do His will (Wis viii 4, ix 9–10), and thus to lead men to life (Prov iv 13, viii 32–35; Sir iv 12; Bar iv 1) and to immortality (Wis vi 18–19). This is precisely the function of Jesus as revealer, as portrayed in numerous passages in John.[16]

This is also the function of Jesus as revealer as portrayed in numerous passages in Thomas. There are sayings in Thomas, many of which have synoptic parallels, which are Jesus' instructions on proper ways to please God (e.g., 25, "Love your brother as your soul; keep him as the apple of your eye.") and to do God's will (e.g., 99, "Those here who do the will of my Father, they are my brothers and mother; they will enter the Kingdom of my Father"; and see the proverbial Logia, 31–36). Thomas certainly contains more wisdom sayings, proverbs, and parables than does John. It was by means of these that the Wisdom tradition taught how to do good and please God.

Again, according to Brown,

> in accomplishing her task, Wisdom speaks in the first person in long discourses addressed to her hearers (Prov viii 3–36; Sir xxiv)—so also Jesus takes his stand and addresses men with his discourses, often beginning with "I am. . . ." The symbols that Wisdom uses for the instruction that she offers are symbols of food (bread) and drink (water, wine), and she invites men to eat and drink (Prov ix 2–5; Sir xxiv 19–21; Isa lv 1–3 [God offering His instruction])—so also Jesus uses these symbols for his revelation (John vi 35, 51ff., iv 13–14).[17]

Thomas does *not* contain long discourses of a Johannine type; all the logia in Thomas are short, of the same approximate length as synoptic sayings. This may well indicate that Thomas' sayings are more primitive than John's. To an extent Thomas does have "I am . . ." statements (cf. 77, "I am the light. . . .") but certainly Thomas has far fewer than John. The symbolism in Thomas of drinking, in 108, 28, 13, is similar to that in John, and this will be discussed at greater length in the following chapter. Thomas has a symbolism of eating, but except for the possible connection between eating and living by the Living One in Logion 111 there is little use of the symbolism of eating or of bread in the Johannine sense.

> Wisdom is not satisfied simply to offer her gifts to those who come; she roams the streets seeking men and crying out to them (Prov i 20–21, viii 1–4; Wis vi 16), so also we find the Johannine Jesus walking along, encountering those who will follow him (i 36–38, 43), searching out men (v 14, ix 35), and crying out his invitation in public places (vii 28, 37, xii 44).[18]

This theme is not obvious in Thomas. Here is where the distinction between a sayings collection and a narrative gospel becomes crucial to the theological framework of different documents. Thomas shows Jesus living on earth, speaking, having short exchanges with people. This is as far as a sayings collection can go. Only with the invention of the "gospel" form were narrative elements added to provide a geographical context for Jesus' sayings.

> One of the most important tasks that Wisdom undertakes is to instruct disciples (Wis vi 17–19)—who are her children (Prov viii 32–33; Sir iv 11, vi 18)—so also in John those disciples who are gathered around Jesus are called his little children (xiii 33). Wisdom tests those disciples and forms them (Sir vi 20–26) until they love her (Prov. viii 17; Sir iv 12; Wis vi 17–18) and they become friends of God (Wis vii 14, 27)—so also Jesus purifies and sanctifies his disciples with his word and truth (xv 3, xvii 17) and tests them (vi 67) until he can call them his beloved friends (xv 15, xvi 27).[19]

Here again the distinction between a sayings collection and a narrative gospel is crucial. The human interactions which are present in John's narrative gospel are not capable of being dramatized in a non-narrative form such as Thomas. In Thomas the idea of the disciple as one who becomes a child (21, 22, 37, 46) is definitely present. We shall discuss its particular meaning in Thomas in the next chapter.

> On the other hand, there are men who reject Wisdom (Prov i 24–25; Bar iii 12; En. xlii 2)—so also we see in John many who will not listen when Jesus offers them the truth (viii 46, x 25). For those who reject Wisdom death is inevitable; truth is unattainable; and their pleasure in the things of life is transitory. . . .
> Thus the coming of Wisdom provokes a division; some seek and find (Prov viii 17; Sir vi 27; Wis vi 12) others do not seek and when they change their minds, it will be too late (Prov i 28). The same language in John describes the effect of Jesus upon men (vii 34, viii 21, xiii 33).[20]

In Thomas 28 Jesus sees that human beings are not thirsting and that they seek to go out of the world empty. In Logia 59 and 92 it is implied that persons may well fail to seek and to find. As with John so with Thomas, human beings have options; they may be in poverty, they may find the treasure; they may be in darkness or in light; they may seek and find, or they may fail to do so.

The preceding considerations show that the Gospel of Thomas has striking similarities to Johannine conceptions and that both derive much of their thought and terminology from the Wisdom tradition. Käsemann says, of John, that "In Christ, the end of the world has not merely come near, but is present and remains present continually."[21] So, in Thomas, Jesus can say that the Kingdom is spread upon the earth in answer to the question, "On what day will the Kingdom come?" (113), and can demand that those who look for the end look to the present and see what is directly in front of their faces.

The present possibility of salvation is common to both Thomas and to John. Thomas, in 11, speaks of the fact that "the living will not die" and this is not dissimilar to John's "Everyone who lives and believes in me will not die" (11:26). John 8:52 reads, "If anyone keeps my word he will not taste death," and in Thomas we find in Logion 1, "He who finds the meaning of these words will not taste death." The Jews rephrase Jesus' words to "If anyone keeps my word he will not see death," and Thomas in Logion 111 claims that "he who lives by the Living One will not see death." These are verbally and conceptually similar. Eternal life in Thomas and in John are possibilities in the present for one who lives by Jesus and his words. A number of scholars believe that a *later* redactor added to John's gospel several eschatological reservations lacking in earlier versions; no such reservations are present in Thomas.

Thomas seems to contrast the world of those who do not find God's Kingdom with the world wherein the Kingdom is hidden. John develops a distinction between world and "world" more radically by equating the "world" with those who reject Jesus' words, so that the contrast takes on the cosmological implications of a world of darkness and demonic power which is opposed to the heavenly world of light above. John very occasionally uses world with positive valuation (e.g., 3:16, "God so loved the world. . . ."). Thomas' use of a dual meaning for the word world can allow him to speak ironically in Logion 110: "He who has found the world and becomes rich [world with positive value], let him deny the world [world with negative value]," in a way impossible to the more starkly dualistic Johannine conception. In Logion 43 we find, "By what I say to you, you do not know who I am . . . ," a notion with obvious Johannine overtones (cf. 14:9); 43 continues, "you have become as the Jews"—a usage, as Brown mentions, that "is quite Johannine."[22]

On the one hand Thomas is replete with Johannine concepts, language, and dichotomies, and shares John's origin in Jewish Wisdom speculation—and John's ideas of the present possibility of eternal life and the present existence of the beginning in the end. On the other hand, Thomas is also replete with sayings parallel and similar to sayings in the synoptic gospels but derived from a source or sources other than the synoptic gospels.

Logion 43 is a Johannine commentary (by means of an introductory sequence of phrases) on a synoptic-style saying derived from a non-synoptic source. This might seem to indicate that a person familiar with John's gospel made the commentary, except that Thomas, with at least 114 logia of Jesus and a substantial community of ideas and modes of expression with Johannine Christianity, *has not one logion which is a quotation from the Gospel of John or from the Letters*. This is remarkable indeed.

Brown offers four ways in which he believes the composition of Thomas could have been influenced by Johannine ideas and vocabulary, other than by use of the Gospel of John (a use that he recognizes is ruled out by the complete absence of quotations from John). I shall consider each of these four, but not in his order.

1) "The author(s) of GTh may have read John in the past and have been influenced, consciously or unconsciously, by recollections."[23] Should we presume, however, that someone with access to a very early sayings source independent of the synoptic gospels had direct access to that source but not to the Gospel of John or to the synoptic gospels, and so had to rely on recollections? It is difficult to believe that one who does *not* consciously or unconsciously reflect in his writing influences he may have picked up from reading Matthew, Mark, or Luke would reflect such influences from John. The particular ideas and modes of expression of Matthew, Mark, and Luke are not in Thomas, although Thomas contains many of the sayings they used. It is also difficult to believe that one who knew only John's Gospel would be interested in the preservation of synoptic style sayings in a way that the author of the Gospel of John certainly was not. Johannine traits are common in Thomas but are by no means ubiquitous. There are numerous sayings in Thomas devoid of Johannine ideas or vocabulary.

2) "The author(s) of GTh may have drawn on a source which in turn drew on John."[24] This is highly unlikely. It would require a conflux, in Thomas, of very badly preserved Johannine traditions and very well preserved "synoptic" traditions. The motivation for the creation of a set of short (and thereby atypical), badly preserved sayings traditions from the Gospel of John is hard to imagine. If we presume that there is a chain from John (the latest Gospel by most estimations) to a source which drew on John and thence to Thomas which draws on that source to produce a *logoi sophon* sayings collection, we must contend with an exact reversal of known literary trends in early Chris-

tianity. We have also multiplied entities needlessly, and are still faced with the fact that Thomas contains no quotations whatsoever from John's gospel.

3) "GTh and John may both be drawing on a third source like Bultmann's hypothetical Offenbärungsreden source."[25] If this were the case, the hypothetical source was very different for the authors of John and Thomas (the lack of direct quotations is again relevant). The former found therein poetic discourses and the latter short and rather enigmatic sayings and brief exchanges. This would, it seems, really require there to be two sources, one used by John and one used by Thomas. The Thomas source would be a sub-set of Thomas logia, yet no non-synoptic logia make more sense when abstracted from Thomas than they do in the document as it stands.

4) "The author(s) of GTh may have had some familiarity with memories of the oral preaching that underlay the Fourth Gospel."[26] This suggestion is similar to the last mentioned if we assume there must have been two Offenbärungsreden sources, the one used by Thomas composed of short logia. If such a source existed, it might well have derived from "the oral preaching that underlay the Fourth Gospel." What would such oral preaching be like? Presumably, it would have been conducted in part by means of short logia of Jesus. It probably would have been more closely connected with the traditions of the words of Jesus that we find in the synoptics than is the Gospel of John, for I assume that John and the synoptics are more divergent in their present forms than was the oral preaching of their respective communities in earlier times.

If we assume that the sayings of Jesus in the Gospel of John were in part derived from sayings of Jesus such as are found in the synoptics, then the oral preaching of the early Johannine community must have contained sayings of Jesus modified in a Johannine way, but less modified than the sayings now preserved in John. One would expect then that a document which remained from the period of the oral preaching of the Johannine communities and which Thomas used would have been a sayings collection, as Thomas is. It probably would have contained some sayings closer to synoptic sayings than are the discourses in John, and would show signs of early development of the Johannine tendencies, including the creation of "I am . . ." sayings, the presentation of Jesus as Wisdom in *sarx*, exploration of such dualities as light and darkness, dual use of the word "world," etc.

In fact, if we try to imagine what a sayings collection underlying Thomas from an early stage of the Johannine community would look like, it would look very much like Thomas itself. Indeed, the hypothesis that the Gospel of Thomas is a sayings collection from an early stage of the Johannine communities accounts for the fact that Thomas contains no quotations from the as yet unwritten Gospel and Letters of John, accounts for the use of both Johannine vocabulary and synoptic-style sayings, and to a certain extent accounts for the fact that the ideas of Thomas are less well conceptualized than the ideas in John.

The connection between Thomas and John is multifaceted and complex. The Christology of Thomas shares with that of John a place of origin in the Jewish Wisdom tradition. Thomas shows familiarity with Johannine vocabulary and ideas, and uses some of the same dichotomies, such as between "world" and world, and between light and dark. It is incorrect to claim that Thomas is wholly a product of the Christianity that produced the Gospel of John. There are ideas in Thomas that do not appear in John, and vice versa. It may, however, be correct to see in the later Johannine writings a developed and transformed version of Thomasine Christianity. Thomas may have been utilized in early Johannine preaching, before Johannine Christianity reached its full development and before the detachment of the Johannine trajectory from the synoptic trajectory took place.

CHAPTER SEVEN

Thomas and Baptism

Because the Gospel of Thomas has a communal audience in mind (cf. 3, 46, 50, etc.), it is not simply a series of sayings for use in private contemplation. Nor does Thomas show any signs that it was intended to be used in preaching to non-Christian audiences. It quite evidently had a function within a community of Christians.

In his article, "The Garments of Shame," Jonathan Z. Smith considers Logia 37 and 21 and concludes that these sayings, or rather, elements of these sayings, stem from Christian baptismal practice and so had their function in relation to that important event in Christian community life.[1] The two logia read as follows:

37 His disciples said, "On what day will you be revealed to us and on what day will we see you?"

Jesus said, "When you undress without being ashamed, and you take your clothes and put them under your feet as little children and tramp on them, then you will see the Son of the Living (One) and you will not fear."

21a Mary said to Jesus, "Whom are your disciples like?"

He said, "They are like little children; they settle themselves in a field that is not theirs. When the owners of the field come, they (the owners) say, 'Give us our field.' They undress before them and release it (the field) to them and give back their field to them." [This logion continues with several further passages to which Smith does not refer.]

Logion 37 has four basic elements in Smith's analysis: (1) the undressing of the disciples, (2) their being naked and unashamed, (3) their treading upon the garments, and (4) their being as little children. "In the light of these," writes Smith, "I would suggest that the origin of Logion 37 is to be found within archaic Christian baptismal practices and attendant interpretation of Genesis 1–3."[2]

Smith finds that texts making reference to Jewish proselyte baptism often mention the nudity of the candidate. He further finds that nudity is common in early Christian iconography of figures who are to be considered types of the resurrection (and hence, baptism). A substantial number of ancient Christian texts refer to baptismal nudity.[3] "Linked to the theme of the initiant's nakedness at baptism," writes Smith, "is the additional element that he be unashamed," and this too is attested frequently in texts.[4]

Both the Western and the Eastern churches associated ritual disrobing with the primal nudity of Adam and Eve. Because Adam and Eve were subsequently clothed in "garments of skin," clothing was thought emblematic of the fallen state. "Old" garments were shed as symbolic of "old" and sinful life and trampled underfoot, an action performed in allusion to Gen. 3:15 where the serpent, sin, is trampled upon. This imagery was present in the African, Spanish, and Syrian ceremonies of exorcism, wherein either sackcloth or garments of goatskin were placed underfoot.[5] While such ceremonies are evidenced in texts later than the first century, they probably indicate a tradition of considerable antiquity.

Smith believes that

> the symbolism of the rite is probably to be traced back to Jewish exegesis of Gen 3:21, the clothing of Adam and Eve by God with "tunics of skins." Some rabbis interpreted this to mean that before the expulsion from Eden, Adam and Eve had bodies or garments of light, but that after the expulsion they received bodies of flesh, or a covering of skin. . . . [The] exegetical tradition regarding the bodies of light and skin in Samaritan, Christian and Gnostic sources allows us to assume an early date and wide diffusion of this motif.[6]

The passage in the Gospel of Thomas, Logion 37, "When . . . you take your clothes and put them under your feet as little children and tramp on them" derives from this Adamic typology, but here it is clearly in an unelaborated state. Nowhere does Thomas claim that clothing is the human physical body.

Despite the fact that he allegorizes Thomas' "clothing" into "fleshly bodies," it is possible to agree in general with Smith when he writes,

> in Christian baptismal symbolism . . . a nexus is established between the taking off of one's clothing at baptism, which symbolizes the unashamed nudity of the first pair, and the treading upon the goatskin, which signifies a triumph over the fleshly bodies with which the primal pair were clothed following the Fall.[7]

It is also easy to concur with him that "there is no need to labor the point that the newly baptized are frequently referred to or conceived of as little children. This metaphor is present within the rites of Jewish proselyte 'baptism,' within the Hellenistic mysteries, as well as in early Christian material."[8] This metaphor too is part of a general Adamic typology, for the little child, the baptized person, was thought to be as innocent and sinless as Adam and Eve were before the fall. Such innocence, it should be made clear, has not to do only with sexuality. As Isa. 7:16 shows, little children were considered to be ignorant of the distinction between good and evil generally. From the viewpoint of Adamic typology, they had not yet eaten from the tree of knowledge of good and evil. One who is like prelapsarian Adam has knowledge neither of the distinction of sexes nor of the fatal distinction between good and evil. Paul may refer to this state of the little child when he says of himself, "there was a time when, in absence of law, I was fully alive" (Rom. 7:9).

Smith summarizes his conclusions in reference to Logion 37 as follows:

> With the exposition of these four elements (nudity, being un-ashamed, treading upon one's garments, and being as little children), it is possible to return to the exegesis of the Gospel

of Thomas Logion 37. The logion is set in the context of an eschatological question: "When will you be revealed to us and when will we see you?" (cf. G.T., Log. 51 and 113). In the Gospel, the language used to describe the disciple in relation to the fulfilled experience of the Kingdom is in terms which suggest a restoration of the ruptured relations following the fall.[9]

As we have seen, the Gospel of Thomas has a major theme which has to do with return to the primordial beginning, in terms of Genesis, the time before the fall.

Smith continues:

> The disciples shall not taste death (G.T. Logia 1, 18, 19, and 85) nor see death (Log. 111); they will be filled with light (Log. 61) and they will reign over the All (Log. 2). More generally, there is an over-all equation of Beginning and End (Log. 18). While it is impossible and indeed illegitimate, as it is in the New Testament, to separate the "realized" and the "futuristic," the "anthropological" and the "cosmological" aspects of the eschatology of the Gospel of Thomas, it is clear that to some degree the disciple, insofar as he is saved, is a New Adam and that the cosmos, insofar as it is redeemed, will be a New Eden. Thus the disciple is called upon to transfigure himself, to appear naked and unashamed; to transcend himself, trampling on the fleshly sinful garments of the Old Man; and to become reborn, to be as a little child.[10]

When he turns to consider Logion 21, Smith concurs with H.M. Schenke's interpretation of the "field" which the disciples return to its proper owners by disrobing as "the cosmos, and the owners (of the field) as the *archontai*."[11] This imagery is quite close to that of Col. 2:15, "On that cross he (Jesus) discarded the cosmic powers and authorities like a garment." (N.E.B.) Since the author of Colossians is speaking of baptism (cf. 2:12) and of the Christian's recapitulation of Christ's activities in death and resurrection (2:12–13), it does not press the passage far to presume that the Christian imitates Christ in discarding his garments and in so doing discarding the "cosmic powers and authorities." In baptism, as one undresses oneself from such powers, one leaves them what is theirs and returns to what is one's own.

Smith believes that in Logion 37 "It is the anthropological dimension of the theology of baptism which is in the foreground; in Logion 21 it is the cosmological."[12] I agree with Smith's conclusion, and refer the reader to his article for more lengthy discussion of these matters.

In Thomas there are three other sayings which refer to the Christian as child, 4, 22 and 46. These sayings are complex in themselves and in their relationships with the synoptic tradition. The first of these, and its context, is:

4a The man old in his days will not hesitate to ask a baby of seven days about the place of life, and he will live.

4b For many who are first shall be last, and they shall become a single one.

5 Know what is in front of your face, and what is concealed from you will be revealed to you. For there is nothing concealed which will not be manifest.

We can see at the outset that 4b is a free-floating saying of Jesus to which has been added a concluding phrase "and they shall become a single one." Becoming single, in the Gospel of Thomas, has to do with the reunification repeatedly advocated within that gospel. The two should become one so that a person subsequently can be undivided and, hence, single. The term "single" seems to be a redactional addition to the end of sayings 16 and 23 as well as here in 4 (cf. Appendix I).

The idea of a baby of *seven* days may have reference to the fact that Jewish proselyte baptism took place seven days after circumcision. The event of circumcision was of greater significance than baptism and was considered the time of rebirth.[13] One reborn after circumcision would be a child of seven days at the time of baptism.

This set of passages (4a–5) has a relationship to the important passage in Matt. 11:25–30:

I thank thee, Father, Lord of heaven and earth, that *thou hast hidden these things from the wise and understanding and revealed them to babes*; yea, Father, for such was thy gracious will. All things have been delivered to me by my Father; and

no one knows the Son except the Father, and no one knows
the Father except the Son and any one to whom the Son
chooses to reveal him. Come to me, all who labor and are
heavy laden and you will find rest for your souls. For my yoke
is easy, and my burden is light. (Emphasis added.)

In this passage Jesus speaks as Wisdom, just as he does in
Thomas' parallel Logion 90, "Come to me because my yoke is
easy and my mastery is gentle and you will find your rest."
Martin Rist wrote that if Matt. 11:25–30 is "considered a liturgical hymn used in connection with Christian baptism, its difficulties of interpretation are largely dissolved."[14] Suggs, aware
of Rist's arguments, concurs with him on other grounds.

It is interesting that 1 Cor. 1–2 is almost universally recog-
nized as furnishing instructive parallels to this passage. Because Paul's whole discussion of the "wise of this world," the
revelation to "babes" and to the "mature," and so on has at
least as its point of departure the issue of baptism, this may
provide a more fitting setting than the Eucharist. In fact, the
designation of the recipients of the revelation as "babes" may
in itself point in this direction.[15]

In the early decades of the church, of course, baptism and first
eucharist were not separate events; baptism preceded eucharist
by only minutes or hours. Suggs further elucidates the meaning
of the Matthean passage by reference to the apocryphal text 4
Ezra 12:35:

This is the dream that you saw, and this is its interpretation.
And you alone were worthy to learn this secret of the Most
High. Therefore write all these things that you have seen in
a book, and put it in a hidden place; and you shall teach them
to the wise among your people whose hearts you know are
able to comprehend and keep those secrets.[16]

As Suggs points out, 4 Ezra in 14:40–47 also claims that Wisdom is hidden in written books, "The secret character of the
revelation is emphasized by the unknown alphabet in which the
amanuensis is instructed to write. The twenty-four books are
for public reading but the seventy are reserved for the eyes of

the wise. 'For in them is the spring of understanding, the fountain of wisdom and the river of knowledge' (verse 47)."[17] Suggs concludes that the "wise" of 4 Ezra and the "babes" of the Q saying quoted in Matthew are simply different titles for the elect.

Suggs reaches these conclusions without reference to the Gospel of Thomas Logion 52. In Logion 5, quoted above, we hear that "what is concealed from you will be revealed to you," and in 52 that

> His disciples said to him, "Twenty-four prophets spoke in Israel and all of them spoke about you." He said to them, "You have left the Living One who is before you and you have spoken about the dead."

Logion 108 gives us reason to believe that Jesus, for Thomas, is the fountain of wisdom (cf. 13). A number of scholars have pointed out the relationship between Thomas' twenty-four prophets (cf. Rev. 4:4) and the twenty-four public books mentioned in 4 Ezra. The connection between Thomas 52 and 4 Ezra 14:40–47 permits us to speculate that there is a connection between what is hidden and made manifest in Logion 5 of Thomas and the hidden things revealed in 4 Ezra 12:35, which become manifest as the spring of understanding and the fountain of Wisdom. In Logion 108 it is said that one who drinks from Jesus' mouth will have hidden things revealed to him.

In Matthew 11:27 Jesus says that "everything is entrusted to me by my Father." This is reminiscent of Jesus' assertion in Thomas 61 that "The things from my Father have been given to me." Further, Jesus is said to claim that "no one knows the Son but the Father, and no one knows the Father but the Son and those to whom the Son may choose to reveal him," (Mt. 11:27). Exegetes of this passage sometimes overlook the fact that the early Christian tradition contains ambiguity in the use of the term "son." The distinctions implied by the use of the capital letter "S" are, of course, absent in the Greek. The "son" may be Jesus, but "son" can also denote baptized Christians.

Paul follows a very ancient Aramaic tradition in Galatians 4:6–7 and Romans 8:14–17 when he assures his readers that they are Sons who can say "Abba" of the Father. In fact, in Galatians

Paul says this in a specifically baptismal context, for the fact that one is a Son and can call the Father "Abba" derives from the fact that "in Christ Jesus you are all sons of God through faith. For as many of you as were baptized into Christ have put on Christ," (Gal. 3:26–27). In the synoptic tradition we find, in Luke, that Jesus said:

> Love your enemies, and do good, and lend, expecting nothing in return; and your reward will be great, and you will be sons of the Most High; for he is kind to the ungrateful and the selfish.

Logion 3b of Thomas reads, "If you know yourselves, then you will be known, and you will know that you are sons of the living Father." Therefore sons know that they are sons of the Father and that the Father knows the sons. That sons can reveal the Father is implicit in Logion 4, for it is the babes who are sons (and elect, and single, etc.) and who are the source of knowledge for "the man old in his days." To them "there is nothing concealed which will not be manifest." The relationship between Thomas 3b to 5 and Matt. 11:25–30 is complex, but for our purposes it is of principal interest that baptism seems to be the *Sitz im Leben* of many of these sayings.

Thomas refers again to the theme of becoming as a child in Logion 46:

> From Adam to John the Baptist, among those born of women, no one is greater than John the Baptist, so that his eyes . . . [here the text is uncertain]. But I said that whoever among you shall become as a child shall know the Kingdom, and he shall become higher than John.

There are parallels to this passage in Matthew (11:11) and Luke (7:28). The passage in Matthew reads, "among those born of women there has risen no one greater than John the Baptist; yet he who is least in the kingdom of heaven is greater than he." Suggs writes that this verse "can hardly mean other than that 'John is born of a woman,' and he who is born 'not of blood nor of the will of man' (John 1:13) or he who is 'born of the water and the Spirit' (John 3:5–8) is greater than he; that is to say, any Christian is greater than John."[18] It is interesting that here, again, imagery of the "child" in Thomas has a relationship to baptism, assuming that John has baptism in mind when he speaks of "water and the Spirit." Brown sees something similar in Matt. 18:3: "I tell you this: unless you turn round and become like children, you will never enter the kingdom of Heaven."[19] The idea (which Suggs credits to Morton Smith) that the passages in John shed light on what it might mean not to be born of woman is interesting. Thomas' Logion 101 may reflect similar imagery, although the crucial concluding saying (101b) is so badly preserved it can only conjecturally be restored. The first half of this logion forms an interesting parallel with Luke 14:26–27 and Matt. 10:37–38 although Matthew's injunction to love one's parents is absent. Thomas 101 reads,

a. He who does not hate his [father] and his mother in my way will not be able to be my [disciple] and he who does [not] love his father and mother in my way, will not be able to be my [disciple],

b. for my mother [according to the flesh gave me death (conjecture: Quispel)] but [my] true [mother] gave me life.

A second mother gives a second birth. Apparently the Gospel of Thomas knows the idea that Christians receive a second birth, a fact also implied by the reiteration of the term "child" for Christians.

Philo may give an important clue to another Thomas saying, one which is significantly different in terminology from 101. Logion 15 reads, "When you see him who was not born of woman, throw yourself down on your face (and) adore him; that one is your father." On the face of it this saying seems incomprehensible. However, Philo might well have understood it. According to Hengel,

in *Quaest. Ex.* 2.29 he [Philo] interprets the statement in 24.2 that Moses alone is allowed to approach God as meaning that the soul, inspired by God with prophetic gifts, 'comes near to God in a kind of family relation, for having given up and left behind all mortal kinds, it is changed into the divine, so that *such men become kin to God and truly divine.*' In *Quaest Ex.*

2.46 Philo calls this transformation a 'second birth,' incorporeal and without involving a mother, brought about through the 'Father of the universe' alone. (Emphasis added.)[20]

The one who in Thomas 15 is "not born of woman" may have been likened to the Father because he has been "changed into the divine" and become "kin to God." This would be in accord with Thomas' terminology for Christians as ones who are "sons of the living Father." Thomas nowhere other than 15 even hints that any person should be considered the Father Himself and so, perhaps, Logion 15 has been garbled in transmission.

On another occasion Thomas speaks of rebirth. Logion 70 reads, "When you beget what is in you, him whom you have, he will save you. If you do not have him in you, he whom you do not have in you will kill you." This saying can be comprehended only if one is sensitive to Thomas' fluctuating terminology. In Logion 3 what is within one is the Kingdom (Wisdom), and in Logion 24 what is within is the light which lights the whole world. Now, in 70, what is within is characterized by a male pronoun. If Jesus may be identified with the light (cf. 77) and the light is within a person (24), presumably the one within is Jesus and the "begetting" is comparable to the "shining" of the light within. This is somewhat reminiscent of the statement in Colossians that the glory of the mystery is "Christ in you." If Jesus is Wisdom, Kingdom is Wisdom, Light is Wisdom, and Wisdom dwells both within persons and within the world, then metaphors of the discovery and manifestation of Wisdom will include finding or seeing the Kingdom, shining forth the Light, and begetting, as in saying 70.

Obviously the terminology in Thomas is not systematic. It shows evidence of different minds grappling with similar problems and expressing them differently (as does, for that matter, the whole New Testament). Regardless of the various terms used, Thomas clearly is concerned with rebirth, with a new begetting. This is consistent with a central concern of Thomas, Christian baptism.

Logion 22 in Thomas is focused on baptism in a particularly interesting way.

22a Jesus saw children being suckled. He said to his disciples, "These children who are being suckled are like those who enter the Kingdom." They said to him, "We are children, shall we enter the Kingdom?"

22b Jesus said to them, "When you make the two one, and when you make the inner as the outer and the outer as the inner and the upper as the lower,

22c so that you will make the male and the female into a single one, so that the male will not be male and the female (not) be female,

22d when you make eyes in the place of an eye, and a hand in place of a hand, and a foot in the place of a foot, (and) an image in the place of an image, then you shall enter [the Kingdom]."

(The divisions here are made for convenience of reference and not because the logion should be considered a collation of four separate sayings.)

Wayne Meeks, in his article "The Image of the Androgyne," discusses what he calls a "baptismal reunification formula" which was familiar to congregations associated with Paul and his school. Reflections of this formula are found in 1 Cor. 12:13, Gal. 3:28, and Col. 3:11. Meeks believes that "a synopsis shows the consistency of the major motifs: baptism into Christ (or, 'one body'), 'putting on Christ' (or, 'the new man'), simple listing of two or more pairs of opposites, and the statement that 'all' are 'one' or that Christ is all."[21]

As Meeks points out repeatedly, these formulas of reunification are not found in isolation from other baptismal motifs. He finds that

reunification follows directly from having "clothed yourselves with Christ" (Gal. 3:28), that is, "the new man" (Col. 3:10). Putting on clothing implies having previously removed clothing, and "putting on" (*enduesthai*) Christ is preceded by having "taken off" (*apekduesthai*) or "laid aside" (*apotithenai*) "the old man" (Col. 3:9; Eph. 4:22)—"the body of flesh" (Col. 2:11). There can be little doubt that the "taking off" and "putting on" is first of all an interpretation of the act of disrobing, which must have preceded baptism, and of the dressing afterward.[22]

As we have seen, in two logia Thomas refers to disrobing in the context of "becoming children," (Logia 21 and 37). The opposites which are reunited are, in part, considered to be sexual according to Meeks:

> The "new man" symbolized by the clothing is the man who is "renewed according to the image of his creator" (Col. 3:10; cf. Eph. 4:24). The allusion to Genesis 1:26–27 is unmistakable; similarly, as we noted earlier, Gal. 3:28 contains a reference to the "male and female" of Gen. 1:27 and suggests that somehow the act of Christian initiation reverses the fateful division of Gen. 2:21–22. Where the image of God is restored, there, it seems, man is no longer divided—not even by the most fundamental division of all, male and female. The baptismal reunification formula thus belongs to the familiar *Urzeit-Endzeit* pattern, and it presupposes an interpretation of the creation story in which the divine image after which Adam was modeled was masculofeminine.[23]

These observations are significant for interpretation of Thomas, especially for Logion 22. There, in 22c, we find an Adamic typology; the divided Adam becomes the primordial and reunified Adam. As Quispel points out,

> according to Philo (cf. b. Erubin 18a, Gen. R. 8, Megillah 9a), the real man, the soul Adam, made after the image of God, is neither male nor female: "But the man who came into existence after the image of God is what one might call an idea, or a genus, or a seal, an object of thought, incorporeal, neither male nor female, by nature incorruptible"[24]

The baptismal initiant is one who makes "a new man," an image in place of an image, and he is thereby "renewed in the Image of his creator." As Paul puts it, with characteristic eschatological reservation, "just as we have borne the image of the man of dust, we shall also bear the image of the man of heaven" (1 Cor. 15:49). Any interpretation of Thomas 22c which is very far from this primitive and Adamic idea of the restoration of the image of God does considerable violence to the simplicity of the text. As J. Z. Smith says, "In the Gospel (of Thomas) the language used to describe the disciple in relation to the fulfilled experience of the Kingdom is in terms which suggest a restoration of the ruptured relations following the Fall."[25] This was generally true for Christians, and the specific locus of such language was the significant event of baptism. Thomas 22d can be understood similarly. Here, however, we must recall that it is the particular emphasis of Paul and his school that the "body of Christ" is the community of Christians. In a strictly Adamic typology the body of Christ will not be distinct from the body of the new Adam, the restored Image of God, and will apply to the individual person who has achieved identification in baptism, not necessarily to the community.

We can hear echoes both of Logion 22 and of Pauline theology in Eph. 2:13–16:

> Now in Christ Jesus you who once were far off have been brought near in the blood of Christ. For he is our peace, who has made us both one, and has broken down the dividing wall of hostility, by abolishing in his flesh the law of commandments and ordinances, that he might create in himself one new man in place of the two, so making peace, and might reconcile us both to God in one body through the cross, thereby bringing the hostility to an end.

The Pauline gospel of annulment of the law, which focuses on the crucifixion and resurrection with concern for communal unity, permeates this passage. But if Meeks is correct, there existed *prior* to Paul's utilization of reunification imagery a primitive "baptismal reunification formula" which did not necessarily have these overtones. Paul, in other words, interpreted the terms of the baptismal liturgy he found already in existence in a more communal and parenetic fashion, focused especially (but not exclusively) on the reunification of Jew and Gentile. In his letters, and in the letters of his followers, there is a series of echoes of earlier liturgical material interpreted in terms of Pauline theology.

Thomas' Logion 22 does not speak of baptism into Christ. Rather, one enters into the Kingdom through baptism or reunification. It is very likely that baptism into the Kingdom is a more primitive idea than the idea of baptism into Christ. It accords much more closely with the ideas of proselyte baptism in

Judaism and with the implications of the baptism of John than does Paul's idea of baptism into Christ. That the two ideas (of baptism into Kingdom and into Christ) are closely related can be seen by reference to Thomas 108 which offers the possibility of union with Jesus. That 108 has baptismal overtones will be demonstrated below.

Thomas apparently knows nothing of the specifics of Pauline theology. This is especially evident in those places where Thomas most clearly reflects the baptismal reunification formula. Thomas never gives any indication of knowledge of baptism as death and resurrection, an idea which surely was one of Paul's major contributions to subsequent Christianity. Still, Paul and Thomas seem to share some ideas regarding baptism derived from common primitive tradition.

For Thomas to say, as in 22d, that one must make parts of the body in place of parts of the body, and to conclude that an image must replace an image, indicates that Thomas was aware of baptism into a new or restored body. This new or restored body is not different than the new or restored image and this new or restored image is not different than the reunification of the androgynous Adam in 22c. As image, body, and Adam are identified with one another in Pauline letters in baptismal contexts, so are they related in Thomas Logion 22.

Within Thomas' context 22b is quite comprehensible. Thomas, it will be recalled, is intent upon stressing the existence of the Kingdom (or Wisdom) of God within persons as well as outside persons. It is spread upon the earth, and it is within you as well as outside of you (cf. 3 and 113). Similarly, in a different metaphoric scheme, light is above all things, within all things, within persons, and brought from within persons to illuminate the whole world (cf. 24 and 77). To say, then, that one must make what is inside, the outside, and outside the inside, and what is above, what is below is nothing but a summary of Thomas' thinking on the pervading locus of the Kingdom and of light. Both are inside, outside, above, and below. The ideal unity of above and below is, in Käsemann's opinion, present in the thought of John. He writes that the "unity between Father and Son is the quality and mark of the heavenly world. It projects itself to the earth in the Word in order to create the community there which, through rebirth from above, becomes integrated into the unity of Father and Son."[26]

It is not the case that Thomas locates the Kingdom within persons exclusively or upon the earth exclusively or that light is located above all things exclusively, within all things exclusively or within persons exclusively. It is the intent of 22b to deny any exclusive location to the Kingdom or Wisdom. In the same vein, Logion 24, following close on Logion 22, says, "His disciples said, 'Show us the place where you are, for it is necessary for us to seek it.' " The request implies that there is an exclusive location to Jesus himself. However, Jesus, as Wisdom, is where Light is. Light in this sense is not an exclusive property of either humans or the world. In Logion 24 Jesus' answer is:

> He who has ears to hear, let him hear. There is light within
> a man of light and he (or, it) lights the whole world. When
> he (or, it) does not shine, there is darkness.

One does not find the light by searching within oneself only, nor by apprehending the world only. One finds the light within oneself illuminating the world. At this point what is inside is outside and what is outside is inside. Paul seems to reflect some of the same idea when he writes, in 2 Cor. 4:6,

> For it is the God who said, "Let light shine out of darkness,"
> who has shone in our hearts to give the light of the knowledge
> of the glory of God in the face of Christ.

Here the locus of Jesus is light within mankind, and this light is related to light present in the creative beginning time.

Logion 22 is a complex compilation of themes which have their place in the symbolism of baptism. Smith's argument allows us to see baptismal symbolism in 22a, and Meeks's argument allows us to see it in 22c in particular, and 22d in general. We find in Logion 22 the idea of the restored image of Adam, no longer male or female. We find there an idea of a new body and of the general reunification of above and below, inside and outside, which derive from Thomas' sophiological speculations

on the locations of Kingdom and light and Wisdom. Thomas'
Logion 22 is a baptismal reunification formula. It is not like such
a formula, nor is it merely derived from such a formula; it is
such a formula. It is not, of course, the only one in early Christian literature.

Thomas' frequent comment that one must make the two one
is a summary of baptismal reunification. It is a mandate for restoration of oneness from duality. The "two" are not any one of
the pairs—body and soul, male and female, above and below,
image and image—in isolation.

It may be that for Thomas to "make the two one" and to
achieve union with Jesus are equivalent demands. Meeks writes
that

> when early Christians in the area of the Pauline mission
> adapted the Adam-Androgyne myth to the eschatological sac-
> rament of baptism, they thus produced a powerful and prolific
> set of images. If in baptism the Christian has again put on the
> image of the Creator, in whom "there is no male and female,"
> then for him the old world has passed away and, behold! the
> new has come.[27]

This makes an excellent summary of Thomas' baptismal theory.
One must, of course, keep in mind the emphasis in Thomas 18
and 19 that he who would stand at the eschatological end must
at the same time stand at the primordial beginning. Then the
world is restored, light dawns, the Kingdom of the Father is
known to have come, and one finds eternal life. It is not difficult
to see that this line of thinking leads toward ideas found in the
Gospel and Letters of John.

Other logia of Thomas fit into a baptismal context. For example, Logion 53 states that

> His disciples said to him, "Is circumcision profitable or not?"
> He said to them, "If it were profitable, their father would
> beget them circumcised from their mother. But the true cir-
> cumcision in the Spirit has found complete usefulness."

The relationship of baptism to symbolic circumcision is attested
early in Col. 2:11:

> In him you were circumcised with a circumcision made with-
> out hands, by putting off the body of flesh in the circumcision
> of Christ; and you were buried with him in baptism, in which
> you were also raised with him through faith in the working of
> God, who raised him from the dead.

And at an earlier time, in Rom. 2:29, Paul wrote that:

> He is a Jew who is one inwardly, and real circumcision is a
> matter of the heart, spiritual and not literal. [or, "directed not
> by written precepts but by the Spirit."]

Significantly, Logion 53 brings the term spirit, uncommon in
Thomas, into relationship with symbolic circumcision. This may
have been a principal theme in the primitive Gentile church.

The spirit is also mentioned in Thomas' Logion 44:

> One who blasphemes the Father, it will be forgiven him, and
> one who blasphemes the Son, it will be forgiven him, but one
> who blasphemes the Holy Spirit, it will not be forgiven him,
> either on earth or in Heaven.

Matthew 28:19 is, of course, the classic location of the baptismal
formula "in the name of the Father and the Son and the Holy
Spirit." The order is the same as in Thomas. This is a later text
in Matthew's Gospel but we do not know how early it may have
been in baptismal liturgy. The importance of the spirit in jux-
taposition to Father and Son is not typical of Thomas. It may be
that the logion was meaningful only in reference to the event of
baptism, wherein the spirit was of particular importance, or it
may mean that Logion 44 is a secondary addition to the text.

One further example should suffice to show the relationship
of the Gospel of Thomas to primitive concepts of baptism. Two
related logia, 13 and 108, each of which speaks of the beneficial
effects of drinking from Jesus, have been considered previously.
Jesus says that because Thomas has drunk from the stream he
measured Thomas need no longer call him master. Jesus proceeds to tell Thomas sayings which the other disciples do not
seem able to understand. In Logion 108 Jesus makes the general statement, directed to no particular person or group, that

He who drinks from my mouth will be as I am, and I will be
he, and the things that are hidden will be revealed to him.

We have already seen that this logion has its roots in the Wisdom tradition wherein Wisdom is likened to a fountain. The
particular symbolism of Logia 13 and 108 occurs in baptismal
context in Paul's first letter to the Corinthians. Paul speaks of
those who

were all under the cloud and all passed through the sea, and
all were baptized into Moses in the cloud and in the sea, and
all ate the same supernatural food and all drank the same
supernatural drink. For they drank from the supernatural Rock
which followed them, and the Rock was Christ. (10:1–4)

This may have reference to the eucharist which in primitive
Christian communities followed immediately upon baptism for
new Christians.

Paul utilizes the same theme in 1 Cor. 12:12–14.

For just as the body is one and has many members, and all
the members of the body, though many, are one body, so it
is with Christ. For by one Spirit we were all baptized into
one body—Jews or Greeks, slaves or free—and all were made
to drink of one Spirit.

Here Paul goes on to discuss the absurdity should feet, ears or
eyes refuse to belong to the body. He refers, of course, to the
church (the body of Christ), but if the body is understood as the
restored image of God, this passage is reminiscent of Thomas
22. Apparently drinking from Christ and drinking from the one
Spirit are, in Paul's mind, two ways of saying the same thing.
The fact that both are mentioned in clearly baptismal contexts
permits us to infer a baptismal context behind Thomas 13 and
108. As noted above, drinking from the mouth of Jesus may
have implied that one received knowledge of hidden things as
well as that one would be able to speak those hidden things.
Thomas is capable of speaking the words Jesus gives him in 13,
but refrains from doing so because the other disciples will fail
to comprehend properly. Paul, in speaking of the one Spirit

poured out for us to drink, is following the train of thought he began in 1 Cor. 12 wherein he lists gifts of the Spirit, among which are "the gift of wise speech," the capacity "to put the deepest knowledge into words," and "the gift of prophecy." These gifts imply both the knowledge of hidden things and the ability to speak those things.

There may be a hidden irony in Thomas 108. If a person is as Jesus is and knows that Jesus is united with him, what are the hidden things which are revealed? It might not be far from Thomas' trend of thought to say that what is hidden and then revealed is the light which is within the images, beneath stones, within persons, and above all things. What is this light, however, but Jesus himself (cf. 77)? If it is Jesus who is within one and who reveals himself, then Thomas 108 brings us into the realm of ideas present in Col. 1:26-27 where the author claims that he came to

> make the word of God fully known, the mystery hidden for ages and generations but now made manifest to his saints. To them God chose to make known how great among the Gentiles are the riches of the glory of this mystery, which is Christ in you, the hope of glory.

Thomas, of course, does not apply an eschatological reservation. He does seem to have the idea that the secret is indeed "Christ in you." Günther Bornkamm has written that

> in Col. 1:27 the content of the mysterion is stated in the formula *Christos en humin*. That is to say, it consists in the indwelling of the exalted Christ "in you" the gentiles.[28]

As elsewhere in Pauline letters, the use of the term "Christ" here is similar to the use of the term "Kingdom" in Thomas (e.g., Log. 3).

We saw, above, that Paul spoke of drinking from Christ in a baptismal context which included eating (1 Cor. 10:2-4), and he may therefore have had in mind some reference to the eucharist. John has a brief passage which is remarkably similar to Thomas 108, and so through Thomas to Paul's reference in First Corinthians.

John 6:56: "He who eats my flesh and drinks my blood abides in me, and I in him."
Thomas 108: "He who drinks from my mouth will be as I am, and I will be he."

These connections deserve careful attention. Coming as they do at points in the New Testament texts which are of major importance for later sacramental theologies, they now carry enormous conceptual weight. It will suffice for our purpose here simply to mention them, so as to draw attention to the probability that the *Sitz im Leben* of Thomas 108 was early Christian liturgical practice.

The sayings in the Gospel of Thomas had a function in early Christian communities connected with the rite of baptism. Thomas is neither a liturgical text itself, nor does it contain very many obviously liturgical passages; only 22 and the ritualized questions and responses of 50 probably played a part in actual baptismal rites.

Thomas' gospel contains few interpretive glosses despite the fact that the sayings therein are varied and enigmatic. For the most part it assumes its audience to be a community rather than individuals alone; but only chaos would have resulted had that community been expected publicly to discover the meaning of the sayings. It is much more likely that the sayings in Thomas were read aloud by one experienced person who then gave a commentary upon them. Thomas would then have been a set of starting-points for instructional discourse, rather than being itself a complete record of instructional discourse.

Thomas is probably part of the post-baptismal instruction of new Christians and was probably read aloud to such persons, with explanations and interpretations added orally for at least the more difficult sayings. Thomas is not, therefore, a purely intellectual document; it is based on a rite, an event, a ritual transformation. To discover the meaning of the sayings, as advocated in Logion 1, is to discover the meaning of the rite. Thomas has no magical conception of baptism as something efficacious apart from one's comprehension of it, any more than Thomas holds that knowing a set of sayings is in and of itself sufficient for salvation.

If Logion 3 is addressed to baptized Christians, it states that all who have been baptized are sons of the Living Father and should be aware of this fact. Thus the self-knowledge advocated by Thomas is probably not self-knowledge by human beings in general but self-knowledge by human beings who have been transformed through baptism. The baptized will know that they are sons of the living Father, that they have come from the light and the Kingdom, into the light and the Kingdom.

CHAPTER EIGHT

Thomas and First Corinthians

If Thomas was a series of sayings utilized as an outline for the instruction of newly baptized Christians, it had two aspects. The first we have in the text of the Gospel of Thomas: the series of logia of Jesus. The second we do not have at all: the interpretations and explanations which were given of the logia. These would vary according to the predilections of the individuals giving the interpretations and explanations.

Paul's first letter to the Corinthians shows that he wrote in opposition to persons whose understanding of Christianity was very much like that of the Gospel of Thomas. There was division in the Corinthian church between Paul's followers and others. The divisions stem, at least in part, from the rite of baptism. Paul writes:

> Each one of you says, "I belong to Paul," or "I belong to Apollos," or "I belong to Cephas," or "I belong to Christ." Is Christ divided? Was Paul crucified for you? Or were you baptized in the name of Paul? I am thankful that I baptized none of you except Crispus and Gaius; lest any one should say that you were baptized in my name. . . . For Christ did not send me to baptize but to preach the gospel, and not with eloquent wisdom, lest the cross of Christ be emptied of its power. (1:12–15, 17)

It is unlikely that Paul baptized his handful of Christians in the name of Paul, and equally unlikely that Cephas did so in his own name. If Apollos engaged in such a practice, Paul could hardly have found himself in such accord with Apollos that he would urge him to return to Corinth (16:12). The divisions are probably not along lines of divergent baptisms but along the lines of divergent *interpretations* of the same baptismal initiation.

Paul, having baptized few, has few in Corinth who were specifically instructed by him regarding the nature of their baptism. He is happy that this is the case because he wishes *all* Christians in Corinth to follow the gospel as he interprets it and not a few. He does not want a party but a wholly Pauline community.

Paul writes to a fairly sizable Christian community. Of those persons he has baptized only a handful. Therefore the great majority have been baptized by other persons, among them Cephas and Apollos. Paul differentiates himself functionally from those others. He came to proclaim the gospel, he writes, not to baptize; he came to proclaim the gospel, not to impress people with his rhetoric. The dichotomy works out thus:

Christ did not send me to baptize

> *But to preach the gospel*

Not with eloquent wisdom

> *Lest the cross of Christ be emptied of its power*

Two things come together here. First, the preaching of the gospel is, according to Paul, the fact of Christ on his cross. Second, the baptizing which Paul does not do has something to do with eloquent wisdom, *sophia logou*. Wisdom plays a key role in Corinth and it is associated, at least in Paul's mind, with baptism.

It is incorrect to argue that there is in Corinth a group of opponents with a single identity against whom Paul wrote his first letter. Paul's letter shows that the Corinthians were divided into a substantial number of factions. Three or perhaps four are named in 1:12 and Paul refers to various groups in 11:18. For this reason I shall not feel free to roam through Paul's letter seeking a hint here and a tidbit there from which to compile a dossier on Paul's opponents. I shall focus primarily upon one unit of the letter, chapters 1–4, wherein the central concern is with the relationship of wisdom to Paul's gospel.

We can tell from 1:17 that Paul associated the *sophia logou* of his opponents with their focus on baptism. As we shall see they oriented themselves toward present fulfillment and it is probable that this fulfillment took place in baptism. What Meeks has called the pre-Pauline "baptismal reunification formula" was revised by Paul and his followers in the direction of future fulfillment and away from present fulfillment. Still, even in Pauline material the present focus of baptismal reunification sometimes comes forth. For example, Col. 3:9 has present orientation and so does Col. 2:9:

> Do not lie to one another, seeing that you have put off the old nature with its practices and have put on the new nature, which is being renewed in knowledge after the image of its creator. Here there cannot be Greek and Jew, circumcised and uncircumcised, barbarian, Scythian, slave, free man, but Christ is all, and in all. (Col. 3:9–11) (cf. Thomas 22, 77 etc.)

> For in him the whole fulness of deity dwells bodily, and you have come to fulness of life in him, who is the head of all rule and authority. (Col. 2:9–10)

Paul himself speaks similarly in 2 Cor. 5:17, "Therefore, if any one is in Christ, he is a new creation; the old has passed away, behold, the new has come."

In effect Paul says here that baptized Christians have already come into the Kingdom. For the most part, however, Paul applies an eschatological reservation to his theory of baptism. It seems that an ancient form of the baptismal rite frequently indicated present passage from the old order to the new order, present acquisition of new birth (cf. John. 3:3–4), new creation (cf. 2 Cor. 5:17), renewal of the image of God (cf. Col. 2:11), present acquisition of new birth (cf. John 3:3–4), new creation that such things are inherent in baptism; he simply claims that their full reality lies in the future. Some of Paul's Corinthian opponents did find baptism productive of such conditions in the present. They claimed already to have come into their fortune and their Kingdom, and Paul says, with sarcasm, that he has been left out (cf. 1 Cor. 4:8).

Paul's Corinthian opponents here are not hypothetical quasi-Valentinian proto-gnostics. They are persons who presume that baptism means that "the world, life and death, the present and the future" (3:22) all fully belong to them in the present, while Paul would have them wait until the Lord comes. Paul's opponents in the first four chapters of his first letter to Corinth may have been people who practiced a baptismal liturgy with attendant instruction focusing on the full acquisition of Christian Kingdom and treasure in the present. This instruction was probably given by means of *sophia logou*. Although Paul takes issue with this, it seems obvious that some persons in Corinth believed that Christ did send them to baptize and they did so relying on wise speech (1:17).

We know little about the persons Paul has in mind in chapters 1–4, but we are given three important clues in 4:8. "At the moment," Paul writes of them, "you are completely satisfied (*kekoresmenoi*), you have grown rich (*eploutisate*), and you have begun your reign (*ebasilausate*)." These are three distinct metaphors for present fulfillment, and Paul's opponents apparently applied them to themselves. All three are important to the Gospel of Thomas.

The word *kekoresmenoi* literally means satiated, as with food or drink. The condition of persons prior to their finding Jesus is "emptiness" in Thomas Logion 28, and this "emptiness" is contrasted with "thirsting." Implicitly, the condition of emptiness will be rectified by those who thirst, and those who thirst will be filled. Thomas Logion 13 utilizes this metaphor as well: Jesus tells Thomas that "I am not your master because you drank; you are drunk from the bubbling spring which I measured." "He who drinks from my mouth will be as I am . . . ," Jesus says in Logion 108. In Thomas there is evidently this sequence: emptiness, thirsting, drinking, being full of drink. One cannot take drunkenness in Logion 13 literally, of course; Logion 28 gives drunkenness as the opposite, and not the completion, of thirsting. In First Corinthians Paul twice speaks of drinking in this way, once from Christ (10:3) and once from the Holy Spirit (12:13), and in both instances the drinking takes place in the context of baptism. Those who utilized the Gospel of Thomas could have claimed that they were *kekoresmenoi*, filled and satiated.

Another metaphor for fulfillment in the Gospel of Thomas is "becoming rich." Logia 109 and 110 form an interesting couplet in reference to this motif.

> 109 The Kingdom is like a man who had a treasure [hidden] in his field, and he did not know it. And [after] he died, he left it to his son. His son did not know, he received the field, he sold [it] and he who bought it, he went, while he was plowing, [he found] the treasure. He began to lend money at interest to [whom] he wished.

> 110 He who has found the world and becomes rich, let him deny the world.

As Logion 95 is a direct command by Jesus not to lend money at interest, it is wrong to take the concluding line of 109 literally; it may derive from symbolism in a Rabbinic parable (see p. 10 above). Both 109 and 110 favor finding treasure and riches. Thomas' dual use of the term "world" in 110 can lead to confusion, but clearly finding the world and becoming rich are advocated. Logion 110 is distantly paralleled by 81:

> He who has become rich, let him become king, and he who has power, let him renounce it.

Since, in Logion 2, we read

> The one who seeks must not cease seeking until he finds, and when he finds, he shall be troubled, and if he is troubled, he will marvel, and he will rule over [all things].

reigning, or becoming king are not possibilities rejected by Thomas but are metaphors for fulfillment. Power, however, should be renounced. It is tempting to think of power here in terms of Paul's claim that his gospel is based on power, but our data are too scanty to enable us to draw any conclusion. Thomas certainly urges the seeking and the finding of treasure. Logion 76 says, in a vein similar to 109,

> The Kingdom of the Father is like a merchant who had goods;
> he found a pearl. This was a prudent merchant. He gave up
> (i.e., sold) the goods, he bought the one pearl for himself.
> You also must seek for the treasure which does not perish,
> which abides where no moth comes near to eat, nor worm
> destroys.

Here Thomas identifies finding the pearl with seeking treasure.
Consequently, those who followed the Christian teachings of the
Gospel of Thomas could have claimed that they were rich or in
possession of treasure.

Finally, adherents of the Gospel of Thomas tradition could
claim to be already in possession of the Kingdom or already
reigning, and this is evident throughout. Logion 2, quoted above,
gives the culmination of the process begun by "seeking" as ruling. Logion 22, giving as it does a summary of baptismal reunification in a variety of modes, concludes with "then you shall
enter [the Kingdom]." Baptism in the Gospel of Thomas gave
initiants the right to claim already to be reigning, already in
possession of the Kingdom.

It has been noted that some of Paul's Corinthian opponents
seem to have adopted the title "babes" in reference to themselves and that Paul turns this against them. If this is the case,
this usage could have been derived from sayings such as those
in Thomas. Five times (Logia 4, 21, 22, 37, 46) Thomas uses
such terminology in reference to those who are newly baptized
and have "become children."

It is clear that Paul identified Christ and Wisdom; it is not
entirely clear whether his opponents did or not. Paul is not interested in giving a presentation of his opponents' christological
theories; he criticizes their *methods* and decries their lack of
respect for his gospel of the cross. Paul writes (1:21–24):

> For since, in the wisdom of God, the world did not know God
> through wisdom, it pleased God through the folly of what we
> preach to save those who believe. For Jews demand signs and
> Greeks seek wisdom, but we preach Christ crucified, a stum-
> bling block to Jews and folly to Gentiles, but to those who are
> called, both Jews and Greeks, Christ the power of God and
> the wisdom of God.

In this context it is probable that the Greeks who look for wisdom are Christians who find Paul's gospel of the cross to be foolishness. Throughout the first four chapters of his letter, he speaks in an intra-Christian context in opposition to those whose Christian faith is built upon "human" wisdom.

It may be that when Paul writes that "to those who are called, both Jews and Greeks, Christ the power of God and the wisdom of God" he refers to the grounds on which all of the parties, including Jewish-Christians seeking miracles, and Greek-Christians seeking wisdom, and Pauline Christians following Paul's gospel of the cross, can agree. The Jews would agree that Christ is the power of God, the Greeks would agree that Christ is the wisdom of God. Pauline Christians would accept both. The question is not whether Christ is the wisdom of God but how this properly should be interpreted; whether it should be done in terms of *sophia logou* or in terms of the cross. It seems far more probable that Paul's Greek opponents found his idea that Christ is God's wisdom *because of the cross* foolishness than that they found the idea that Christ is God's wisdom to be foolishness. Only here, in all of his letters, does Paul claim that Christ is the wisdom of God. There seems some reason to believe that ideas like those in Thomas were present in Corinth when Paul wrote his first letter.

The *Sitz im Leben* of the Gospel of Thomas was most probably post-baptismal instruction. It is in the form of sayings of the wise and presents itself as a set of sayings of Jesus who is himself Wisdom. The persons who used Thomas could claim on the basis of it that they were filled or satisfied, that they had become rich, and that they presently reigned in the Kingdom. They regarded themselves as persons who had become babes or children. They spoke of having had the hidden things, the mysteries, revealed to them, as does Paul in I Cor. 4:1. They spoke of the present victory of light over darkness as revelatory and believed that inward motives are now revealed before heaven, while Paul speaks similarly but in a future tense in 4:5. The *Sitz im Leben* of the wisdom Paul opposes is baptism (1:17). He sarcastically characterizes his opponents as being filled or satisfied, being already rich, already reigning in the Kingdom. He seems to imply that they wrongfully pride themselves on being babes. First Corinthians 1–4 is testimony to the antiquity of many of the central ideas in the Gospel of Thomas. It is, of course, impossible to claim that the Gospel of Thomas was actually in use in Corinth.

Conclusion

Thomas is a text from the first century of Christianity. The format of the text, *logoi sophon*, is that of Q (ca. A.D. 50–70) and is reflected in the later synoptic grouping of sayings (e.g., the Sermon on the Mount and Mark 4:1–34). Although later decades of the Christian movement saw the development of resurrection discourses, mythological Sophiology, distinctions between the lower creator god and the true transcendent God, and lengthy dialogues between savior and disciples, these are not present in Thomas. Whether or not one accepts the idea that the form *logoi sophon* was an element in a trajectory leading toward such forms and themes, these later forms and themes do not have anything to do with the Gospel of Thomas. In form it is more like Q than anything else is.

Thomas' sayings are independent of the synoptic gospels and the synoptics do not show any dependence upon Thomas. Still, it is significant that many of Thomas' sayings are paralleled in the synoptics. Thomas' sayings are sometimes in an earlier form than theirs, sometimes the contrary is true. If the synoptic writers, any or all of them, had had access to Thomas they would not have found it totally congenial to their futuristic eschatologies and their emphasis on the cross and resurrection. There may be instances of radical revision of Thomas' sayings in the synoptics, instances where mystagogic sayings have been transformed into parenetic sayings (Logion 22 and Mark 9:42–10:15?, Logion 24 and Matthew 6:22–23 and Luke 11:34–36?, Logia 6 and 14 and Matthew 6:2–18?, Logion 13 and Mark 8:27–30?). As these sayings in their canonical form are so utterly familiar and those in Thomas so seemingly strange it is unlikely that any contemporary critical methodology will provide means to determine *radical* reworking.

The Christology, or Jesusology, of Thomas is complex but it does not stem from decades of Christian theological speculation. It derives from a naive application of manifold Wisdom speculations to Jesus. The lack of Manichean or Marcionite dualism, the absence of any mythology of Sophia's fall or of Christ's ascent or descent through hostile realms populated by inimical Archons indicate that Thomas' sophiological Christology existed prior to or in ignorance of what many call gnosticism.

Thomas has something of the dualism of John, but it has a far more positive view of the world than does John. Thomas has something of the antagonism toward the flesh we find in Paul, but this is less emphatic than in Paul. If Thomas is gnostic in its dualism, John is more so. If Thomas is encratite in its disvaluing of family and social relations, it is so in sayings which are, for the most part, paralleled in the synoptic tradition (e.g., 55 and 99), and we find nothing as "encratite" in Thomas as we find in Luke 9:60–10:15.

What then is the Gospel of Thomas? It is a collection of sayings attributed to Jesus, some authentic and some not. Its background is that of Jewish Wisdom speculation. It is wholly independent of the New Testament gospels; most probably it was in existence before they were written. It should be dated A.D. 50–70.

The Gospel of Thomas is difficult to interpret because it stands at the beginning of Christian theological speculation. It is naive and unsystematic, and hence systematic understanding of it may not be possible. Thomas does not presuppose the Johannine or synoptic gospels or the theology of Paul; even less does it suppose the mythologies of second-century theologians such as Valentinus or Heracleon. In reference to the sayings of Jesus, the synoptic gospels depend upon and incorporate sayings which first circulated in Thomas' and Q's *logoi sophon* format. In reference to baptism, Paul's eschatological reservations may presuppose Thomas' orientation to present fulfillment in baptism. In reference to a dualism of light/dark, world/"world," and to *ego eimi* discourses of Jesus, John may be a later development of what we find here and there in Thomas.

The Gospel of Thomas is a mid-first-century text. It is an early document of sophiological Christianity oriented toward baptismal initiation, and it can be considered gnostic in no meaningful sense. When the time comes that Thomas is understood to have come into being ca. A.D. 50–70, our knowledge of the history of the early church will immeasurably increase.

Appendix I
The Structure of Thomas

The Gospel of Thomas may have originally been divided into four chapters or sections. As these do not show any very significant differences in ideology or style, it is unlikely that they are units of different origin which were later combined. Rather, they are four separable but related chapters.

These four chapters come into view when the text is divided at four of the sayings which have to do with seeking and finding. These form introductory sayings, as do similar sayings in the Wisdom of Solomon (cf. 1:1–2, 6:12–14). After these introductory sayings, in three chapters there shortly appear a series of synoptic-style parables. All chapters then present a series of sayings in no particular order that I can discern, but toward the end of the four chapters there is a series of sayings in much the same order, reflecting several of the following themes in sequence:

- making the two one
- being chosen, solitary, standing
- parables about finding
- light
- renunciation of the world or power
- knowledge of which the world is not worthy
- sayings on body and soul and spirit

Three chapters conclude with a question and answer sequence having to do with the time of the end.

None of the four chapters has all of these elements in perfect sequence, and this may indicate that each has undergone alterations in sayings-order independent of alterations made in the others. The pattern is most apparent if set forth in the form of a chart. The following chart has, in its left hand columns, numbers of the sayings in Thomas, and in its right hand section a précis of sayings, highlighting common features. Thomas' four chapters are:

A: 2–37
B: 38–58
C: 59–91
D: 92–113

A	B	C	D	
2				The one who *seeks* must not cease seeking until he *finds*
	38			You will *seek* me, and you will not *find* me
		59		Lest you die and *seek* to see him and you cannot see
			92	*Search* and you will *find* (94) He who *searches* will *find*
8				
9				Synoptic parables
		63		
		64		Synoptic parables
		65		
			96	
			97	Synoptic parable and others stylistically similar
			98	
21			103	Know when the robbers are coming and gird your loins
22	46			Those like children shall enter the Kingdom
22				When you *make the two one* . . . .
	48			If *two make peace* . . . they shall say to the mountain *"move"*
			106	When you *make the two one* . . . say *"mountain, move"*
23				I shall *choose* you . . . they shall *stand*
	49			Blessed are the *solitary* and the *chosen*

		75	Many are *standing* but the *solitary* will enter
		76	Parable: Kingdom is like a merchant who *found* a pearl You too *seek* for treasure which does not perish
		107	Parable: Kingdom is like a shepherd. He *searched* for the one sheep until he *found* it
24			There is *light* within a man of light and he lights world
	50		We come from the *light*, where the light came through itself
		77	I am the *light* which is above all things
27			If you do not fast from the world you will not find the Kingdom
	54		Blessed are the poor for yours is the Kingdom
		81	Let him who has become rich become king, let him with power renounce it
		110	He who has found the world and becomes rich, let him deny the world
	56		*Know world,* find corpse; find corpse, *world not worthy*
		80	*Know world,* find body; find body, *world not worthy*
		111	*Know self, world not worthy*
29			If the flesh exists because of *spirit* it is a miracle
		87	*Body* wretched depends on body; *soul* wretched depends on two
		112	Woe to *flesh* depends on *soul;* woe to soul depends on flesh
37			On what day will you be revealed to us, on what day will we see?
		91	Tell us who you are so that we can believe in you.
		113	On what day will the Kingdom come?

Both Logia 37 and 113 contain questions about the time of the end; the answer to Logion 91 presupposes a question about the time of the end. Final sayings having to do with the time of the end are a traditional motif of conclusion for collections of Jesus' logia. In the words of J. Robinson,

> the eschatological climax [of the Sermon on the Mount] is the same concluding motif that one can sense in the Didache (chapt. 16), the gospels (Mark 13 par.) and even in Q (Luke 17:20–37).[1]

Mark 13 is an extended answer to the disciples' question, "Tell us . . . when will this happen? What will be the sign when the fulfilment of all this is at hand?" (Mark 13:4). For Thomas the end is not to come; it is already here for those who find it (cf. 37, 91, 113).

I do not wish to press the point of these four chapters. My arguments concerning the Gospel of Thomas as a whole are not effected by their existence or absence. Nevertheless if we, for the moment, assume that these four chapters are real and not illusory, a few interesting observations can be made:

1) Logion 1 becomes even more obviously a comment upon the collection as a whole and not a part of the collection. Someone apparently thought Thomas to be a collection of "secret" sayings and added Logion 1 to the collection at a later stage, when the chapters were combined into a single unified sequence of logia. It may be significant that the incipit of the Nag Hammadi text *Thomas the Contender*, "The secret words which the Savior spoke to Judas Thomas . . . ," is known to be secondary. John Turner writes, "The *incipit* of *Thomas the Contender* constitutes both the designation of the content of the work and its legitimization. That the *incipit* is a later addition is proved by its linguistic features alone."[2]

2) The final Logion 114 can be seen to have been added to the text of Thomas at a later date. This is not dependent on whether we agree that Thomas had four chapters, for much of the terminology of this saying is absent in the rest of Thomas:

a. The saying begins with a disciple, Simon Peter, addressing the other disciples. This literary device is otherwise never used by Thomas.
b. The idea of one "guided" by Jesus occurs only here.
c. In Thomas D we find the phrase "Kingdom of the Father" appearing in 96, 97, 98, 99, 113. Only in 114 is "Kingdom of Heaven" used.
d. Only in 114 do we hear anything like the idea that a person should "become a living spirit."
e. Finally, this logion is in direct contradiction to 22. There *the male should become female,* the female become male and neither should be any longer male or female. Here, in 114 the status "male" is positively valued and the status "female" is negatively valued. Indeed, the woman should become male.

Given Thomas' fluidity of terminology and lack of fully systematic ideology, any one of these discrepancies could be overlooked. There are, however, too many unique and anomalous usages in 114 to allow us to consider it part of the original Gospel of Thomas.

3) *Only* in Thomas chapter A is the expression "he who has ears *to hear,* let him hear" used and it is used three times, 8, 21, 24. In all other places, throughout chapters B, C and D the expression is "he who has ears, let him hear."

4) *Only* in Thomas chapter A do we find the secondary addition of the motif of "singleness" to the final line of logia. Three times this occurs: in Logion 4 "and they shall become a single one"; in 16 "and they shall stand as solitaries"; and in 23 "they are a single one." It is likely that at some point a copyist added these tendentious endings to a version of Thomas A from which they were absent.

5) Logia 5 through 8 show evidence of a very tired scribe. The following seems to have happened:

a. 5 probably ended with "Jesus said, 'Do not lie, and do not do what you hate, because all is revealed before heaven.' " But this was copied after the introductory questions of 6, and then 5 was repeated. The answers to the questions posed in 6 were not copied until the scribe realized his mistake and added them at the beginning of 14.

    b. 7 should give us a parallel structure which concludes once "the lion will become man" and once "the man will become lion." The scribe gives us "the lion will become man" twice.

    c. 8 should begin like all of Thomas' other Kingdom parables with something like "The Kingdom of Heaven (or, of the Father) is like . . ." but begins "the Man is like . . . ."

One may be able to hypothesize tendentious reasons for one or another of these unusual features and apparent errors, but considering that they are all in sequence the greater likelihood is that they are due to scribal error and that the scribe retired for the night upon completion of 8. Because these errors appear in an Oxyrhynchus papyrus, we may suspect that they were made at an early time in the transmission of the text.[3]

It appears to me, and this is simply an intuition, that Thomas' first section is devoted to basic matters as regards baptismal initiation (22 and 37 especially), and this seems appropriate to an initial sequence of sayings. This intuition is reinforced by the reiterated use of the terminology for childhood and infancy in the first section. This terminology is rare elsewhere in Thomas.

There may be a glimmering of sense in the order of Thomas' second section. It can be understood as follows:

    a. 38: An introductory saying regarding seeking and finding.

    b. 39–46: Sayings which present opposing types of persons or behaviors (43 is a distorted version of Luke 6:43).

    c. 47: A collection of sayings demanding choice.

    d. 48–50: Sayings defining proper Christians.

    e. 51–53: Dialogical sayings regarding significant matters: the repose of the dead, the new world, the presence of Jesus, the value of circumcision.

    f. 54–56: Proper modes of behavior: poverty, separation from family, understanding the world and being superior to the world.

    g. 57: The parable of the wheat and the tares, a rather appropriate conclusion which harks back to 40.

And yet the collection, as I define it, concludes with 58, the relationship of which to the whole I do not see.

The rationale for the order of sayings in the third section is wholly opaque to me. Apart from noticing that the fourth section has a concentration of sayings regarding wealth and family, and that the concluding logion 113 seems fittingly to refer back to the principal statement of 3, the order of the Gospel of Thomas' fourth section escapes me.

At times it seems to me that whoever put the document together must surely have done it in what he or she thought a proper and rational order. On the other hand, we can see from the Oxyrhynchus papyri that some (although not overmuch) alteration in sayings order occurred in the process of textual transmission. I look forward to the time when someone unambiguously uncovers the secret to Thomas' order or, indeed, to the time when we can conclude that the sayings are essentially random, for that seemingly discouraging result would in fact be a negative conclusion of considerable interest and significance.

Appendix II
A Translation of the Gospel of Thomas

by David R. Cartlidge
*copyright © 1980 by David R. Cartlidge and David
L. Dungan.*
Used by permission of Fortress Press.

There are many translations of the Gospel of Thomas, most of which are quite competently done. I have chosen to use that of David Cartlidge not because his differs from most in any major ways in interpretation, but because he has a pleasant English style, free from the cuteness and archaisms which some feel appropriate to any translation of an ancient Christian text. He also avoids the over-literalism and the tendency to retain Coptic sentence structure which occasionally appear in other translations. David Cartlidge has had nothing whatsoever to do with the writing of the present book.

At one point only do I differ with the translation to the extent that I feel it must be altered. This regards the word that Cartlidge and others render as "the All" or, once (77) as "all of them." The "All" is not an English word, as capitalized, but a technical gnostic term which translators insert into the text. Accordingly, I prefer the use of "all things" to "the All." It seems to me that "all things" is appropriately neutral.

(The division of the text into four sections, a prologue and an added saying is made by S. Davies.)

Prologue

These are the secret words which the living Jesus spoke and Didymos Judas Thomas wrote them down.

1.   And he said, "He who finds the meaning of these words will not taste death."

Section One

2.   Jesus said, "The one who seeks must not cease seeking until he finds, and when he finds, he shall be troubled, and if he is troubled, he will marvel, and he will rule over the All." (Change "the All" to "all things"?)

3.   Jesus said, "If the ones who lead you say, 'There is the kingdom, in heaven,' then the birds will go first before you into heaven (or—the birds of heaven shall go before you). If they say to you, 'It is in the sea,' then the fish shall go before you. Rather, the kingdom is within you and outside you. If you know yourselves, then you will be known, and you will know that you are sons of the living Father. But if you do not know yourselves, then you are in poverty and you are poverty."

4.   Jesus said, "The man old in his days will not hesitate to ask a baby of seven days about the place of life, and he will live. For many who are first shall be last, and they shall become a single one."

5.   Jesus said, "Know what is in front of your face, and what is concealed from you will be revealed to you. For there is nothing concealed which will not be manifest."

6.   His disciples asked him, "Do you want us to fast, and how shall we pray, and shall we give alms, and what food regulations shall we keep?" Jesus said, "Do not lie, and do not do what you hate, because all is revealed before Heaven. For nothing is hidden that shall not be revealed, and nothing is covered that shall remain without being revealed."

7.   Jesus said, "Blessed is the lion which the man shall eat, and the lion will become man; and cursed is the man whom the lion shall eat, and the lion will become man."

8. And he said, "The Man is like a wise fisherman who threw his net into the sea. He drew it up from the sea; it was full of small fish. The fisherman found among them a large, good fish. He threw all the small fish back into the sea; he chose the large fish without regret. He who has ears to hear, let him hear."

9. Jesus said, "Behold, the sower went out; he filled his hand; he threw. Some fell on the road. The birds came; they gathered them up. Others fell on the rock and did not send roots into the earth and did not send ears up to heaven. Others fell among thorns. They choked the seed and the worm ate them (i.e., the seed). And others fell on good earth, and it raised up good fruit to heaven. It bore sixty measures and one hundred-twenty measures."

10. Jesus said, "I have thrown fire on the world, and behold, I guard it until it is on fire."

11. Jesus said, "This heaven will pass away and your heaven above it will pass away, and the dead do not live, and the living will not die. In the days when you ate the dead, you made it alive; when you come into the light, what will you do? On the day when you were one, you became two. But when you have become two, what will you do?"

12. The disciples said to Jesus, "We know that you will go away from us; who will become great over us?" Jesus said, "To whatever place you have come, you will go to James the righteous; heaven and earth came into being for him."

13. Jesus said to his disciples, "Make a comparison and tell who I am like." Simon Peter said to him, "You are like a righteous angel." Matthew said to him, "You are like a wise man." Thomas said to him, "Master, my mouth will not be able to say what you are like." Jesus said, "I am not your master because you drank; you are drunk from the bubbling spring which I measured." And he took him; he went aside. He spoke to him three words. When Thomas returned to his companions, they asked him, "What did Jesus say to you?" Thomas said to them, "If I tell you one of the words which he said to me, you will pick up stones; you will throw them at me. And fire will come from the stones and consume you."

14. Jesus said to them, "If you fast, you will bring sin upon

yourselves and, if you pray, you will condemn yourselves, and, if you give alms, you will do evil to your spirits. And if you enter any land and wander through the regions, if they receive you, whatever they set before you, eat it. Heal the sick among them. For that which goes in your mouth will not defile you, but that which comes out of your mouth is what will defile you."

15.   Jesus said, "When you see him who was not born of woman, throw yourself down on your face (and) adore him; that one is your father."

16.   Jesus said, "Men might think I have come to throw peace on the world, and they do not know that I have come to throw dissolution on the earth; fire, sword, war. For there shall be five in a house: three shall be against two and two against three, the father against the son and the son against the father, and they shall stand as solitaries."

17.   Jesus said, "I will give you what no eye has seen and what no ear has heard and no hand has touched and what has not come into the heart of man."

18.   The disciples said to Jesus, "Tell us in which way our end will occur." Jesus said, "Have you found the beginning that you search for the end? In the place where the beginning is, there the end will be. Blessed is he who will stand at the beginning, and he will know the end and he will not taste death."

19.   Jesus said, "Blessed is he who was before he was created. If you become my disciples (and) you hear my words, these stones shall serve you. For you have five trees in paradise which do not move in summer or winter and they do not shed their leaves. Whoever knows them shall not taste death."

20.   The disciples said to Jesus, "Tell us, what the Kingdom of Heaven is like?" He said to them, "It is like a mustard seed, smaller than all seeds. But when it falls on plowed ground, it puts forth a large branch and becomes a shelter for the birds of heaven."

21.   Mary said to Jesus, "Whom are your disciples like?" He said, "They are like little children; they settle themselves in a field that is not theirs. When the owners of the field come, they (the owners) say, "Give us our field." They undress before them and release it (the field) to them and give back their field to

them. Because of this I say, if the owner of the house knows that the thief is coming, he will watch before he comes and will not let him break into his house of his kingdom and carry away his goods. But you watch especially for the world; gird your loins with great power lest the robbers find a way to come upon you, because the thing you expect, they will find. Let there be a man of understanding among you. When the fruit ripened, he came quickly, his sickle in his hand (and) he reaped it. He who has ears to hear, let him hear."

22. Jesus saw children being suckled. He said to his disciples, "These children who are being suckled are like those who enter the Kingdom." They said to him, "We are children, shall we enter the Kingdom?" Jesus said to them, "When you make the two one, and when you make the inner as the outer and the outer as the inner and the upper as the lower, so that you will make the male and the female into a single one, so that the male will not be male and the female (not) be female, when you make eyes in the place of an eye, and hand in place of a hand, and a foot in the place of a foot, (and) an image in the place of an image, then you shall enter [the Kingdom]."

23. Jesus said, "I shall choose you, one from a thousand, and two from ten thousand, and they shall stand; they are a single one."

24. His disciples said, "Show us the place where you are, for it is necessary for us to seek it." He said to them, "He who has ears to hear let him hear. There is light within a man of light and he (or, it) lights the whole world. When he (or, it) does not shine, there is darkness."

25. Jesus said, "Love your brother as your soul; keep him as the apple of your eye."

26. Jesus said, "The chip that is in your brother's eye you see, but the log in your own eye you do not see. When you take the log out of your eye, then you will see to remove the chip from your brother's eye."

27. "If you do not fast (in respect to) the world, you will not find the Kingdom; if you do not keep the Sabbath a Sabbath, you shall not see the Father."

28. Jesus said, "I stood in the midst of the world, and I

appeared to them in the flesh. I found all of them drunk; I did not find any of them thirsting. And my soul was pained for the sons of men because they are blind in their heart, and they do not see that they came empty into the world; they seek to go out of the world empty. However, they are drunk. When they have shaken off their wine, then they shall repent."

29.   Jesus said, "If the flesh exists because of spirit, it is a miracle, but if spirit (exists) because of the body, it is a miracle of miracles. But I marvel at how this great wealth established itself in this poverty."

30.   Jesus said, "Where there are three Gods, they are Gods; where there are two or one, I am with him."

31.   Jesus said, "A prophet is not acceptable in his own village; a physician does not heal those who know him."

32.   Jesus said, "A city they build and fortify upon a high mountain cannot fall, nor can it be hidden."

33.   Jesus said, "What you hear in your ear, preach in [others'] ear[s from] your housetops. For no one kindles a lamp and puts it under a basket, nor does he put it in a hidden place, but he sets it on a lampstand so everyone who comes in and goes out will see its light."

34.   Jesus said, "If a blind man leads a blind man, the two of them fall into a pit."

35.   Jesus said, "It is impossible for one to enter the house of the strong man and rob it violently, unless he bind his hands; then he shall pillage his house."

36.   Jesus said, "Do not be anxious from morning to evening and from evening to morning about what you will put on yourselves."

37.   His disciples said, "On what day will you be revealed to us and on what day will we see you?" Jesus said, "When you undress without being ashamed, and you take your clothes and put them under your feet as little children and tramp on them, then you will see the Son of the Living (One) and you will not fear."

Section Two

38.   Jesus said, "Many times you desired to hear these words which I say to you and you have no one else from whom to hear them. There will be days when you will seek me, and you will not find me."

39.   Jesus said, "The Pharisees and the Scribes took the keys of knowledge; they hid them. They did not enter, and they did not allow to enter those who wanted to enter. But you be wise as serpents and as innocent as doves."

40.   Jesus said, "A vine was planted without the Father and it has not strengthened; it will be pulled up by its roots (and) it will rot."

41.   Jesus said, "He who has in his hand, it shall be given to him; and he who does not have, even the little he has shall be taken away from him."

42.   Jesus said, "Be wanderers."

43.   His disciples said to him, "Who are you that you say these things to us?" "By what I say to you, you do not know who I am, but you have become as the Jews. They love the tree, they hate its fruit; they love the fruit, they hate the tree."

44.   Jesus said, "One who blasphemes the Father, it will be forgiven him, and one who blasphemes the Son, it will be forgiven him, but one who blasphemes the Holy Spirit, it will not be forgiven him, either on earth or in Heaven."

45.   Jesus said, "They do not pick grapes from among thorns, nor do they gather figs from among camel's thistles; they do not give fruit. F[or a go]od man brings forth good fr[om] his treasure; a b[ad] man brings forth evil from his evil treasure in his heart, and he speaks evil. For out of the abundance of his heart, he brings forth evil."

46.   Jesus said, "From Adam to John the Baptist, among those born of women, no one is greater than John the Baptist, so that his eyes . . . [here the text is uncertain]. But I said that whoever among you shall become as a child shall know the Kingdom, and he shall become higher than John."

47.   Jesus said, "A man cannot mount two horses; he cannot stretch two bows. A servant cannot serve two masters; either he

will honor the one and the other he will scorn. . . . No man drinks old wine and right away wants to drink new wine; and they do not put new wine into old wineskins lest they tear, and they do not put old wine into new wineskins lest it spoil it. They do not sew an old patch on a new garment, because there will be a tear."

48. Jesus said, "If two make peace between themselves in the same house, they shall say to the mountain, 'Move away,' and it will be moved."

49. Jesus said, "Blessed are the solitary and the chosen, because you will find the Kingdom; because you come from it, you will again go there."

50. Jesus said, "If they say to you, 'Where did you come from?' say to them, 'We come from the light, where the light came through itself. It stands [. . .] and reveals itself in their image.' If they say to you, '(who) are you?' say to them, 'We are his sons and we are the chosen of the living Father.' If they ask you, 'What is the sign of your Father who is in you?' say to them, 'It is a movement and a rest.' "

51. His disciples said to him, "When will be the rest of the dead and when will the new world come?" He said to them, "What you look for has come, but you do not know it."

52. His disciples said to him, "Twenty-four prophets spoke in Israel and all of them spoke about you." He said to them, "You have left the Living One who is before you and you have spoken about the dead."

53. His disciples said to him, "Is circumcision profitable or not?" He said to them, "If it were profitable, their father would beget them circumcized from their mother. But the true circumcision in the Spirit has found complete usefulness."

54. Jesus said, "Blessed are the poor, for yours is the Kingdom of Heaven."

55. Jesus said, "He who does not hate his father and his mother cannot be my disciple and (he who) does not hate his brothers and his sisters and (does not) carry his cross in my way will not be worthy of me."

56. Jesus said, "He who has known the world has found a

corpse, and he who has found a corpse, the world is not worthy of him."

57.   Jesus said, "The Kingdom of the Father is like a man who had (good) seed. His enemy came by night, he sowed a weed among the good seed. The man did not let them pull up the weed. He said to them, 'Lest you go and pull up the weed and you pull up the wheat with it.' For on the day of the harvest the weeds will appear; they will pull them up and burn them."

58.   Jesus said, "Blessed is the man who has suffered; he has found the Life."

Section Three

59.   Jesus said, "Look upon the Living One as long as you live, lest you die and seek to see him and you cannot see."

60.   (They saw) a Samaritan carrying a lamb; he was going to Judea. He said to his disciples, "Why does he carry the lamb?" They said to him, "That he may kill it and eat it." He said to them, "As long as it is alive he will not eat it, but (only) if he has killed it and it has become a corpse." They said, "Otherwise he cannot do it." He said to them, "You yourselves seek a place for yourselves in rest, lest you become a corpse and be eaten."

61.   Jesus said, "Two will be resting on a couch; the one will die, the one will live." Salome said, "Who are you, man? As if from the One (?) you sat on my couch and you ate from my table." Jesus said to her, "I am He Who Is, from Him Who is the Same. The things from my Father have been given to me." (Salome said,) "I am your disciple." (Jesus said to her,) "Therefore, I say, if anyone should be the same (lit., deserted) he will be filled with light, but if he is divided, he will be filled with darkness."

62.   Jesus said, "I tell my mysteries to those who are worthy of my mysteries. What your right (hand) will do, do not let your left (hand) know what it does."

63.   Jesus said, "There was a rich man who had many goods. He said, 'I will use my goods so that I will sow and reap and

plant and fill my warehouses with fruit so that I will not be in need of anything.' He said this in his heart. And in that night he died. He who has ears, let him hear."

64. Jesus said, "A man had guests and when he had prepared the banquet, he sent his servant to invite the guests. He went to the first; he said to him, 'My master invites you.' He said, 'Money is owed me by some merchants. They will come to me in the evening; I will go and I will give them orders. Please excuse me from the dinner.' He went to another; he said to him, 'My master invited you.' He said to him, 'I bought a house and they ask me (to come out) for a day (to close the deal). I will not have time.' He went to another, he said to him, 'My master invites you.' He said to him, 'My friend is going to marry and I will prepare a dinner; I will not be able to come. Please excuse me from the dinner.' He went to another; he said to him, 'My master invites you.' He said to him, 'I have bought a town, I go to collect the rent. I will not be able to come. Please excuse me from the dinner.' The servant returned; he said to his master, 'Those whom you invited asked to be excused from the dinner.' The master said to his servant, 'Go outside to the streets, bring those whom you find so that they may feast.' Buyers and merchants will not enter the places of my Father."

65. He said, "A good man had a vineyard. He gave it to some farmers so that they would work it and he would receive its profits from them. He sent his servant so that the farmers would give him the profits of the vineyard. They seized his servant, they beat him and almost killed him. The servant went back; he told his master. His master said, 'Perhaps he did not know them.' He sent another servant. The farmers beat the other one. Then the master sent his son. He said, 'Perhaps they will respect my son.' Those farmers seized him, they killed him, since they knew he was the heir of the vineyard. He who has ears, let him hear."

66. Jesus said, "Show me the stone which those who built rejected. It is the cornerstone."

67. Jesus said, "He who knows the All, but lacks (i.e., does

not know) himself, lacks everything." (Change "the All" to "all things"?)

68. Jesus said, "Blessed are you when they hate you and persecute you, and no place will be found where you have [not] been persecuted."

69a. Jesus said, "Blessed are those whom they persecuted in their heart; these are they who knew the Father in truth."

69b. "Blessed are those who are hungry, so that the belly of him who hungers will be filled."

70. Jesus said, "When you beget what is in you, him whom you have, he will save you. If you do not have him in you, he whom you do not have in you will kill you."

71. Jesus said, "I shall destroy [this] house and no one will be able to build it [again]."

72. [A man] s[aid] to him, "Speak to my brothers so that they shall divide my father's possessions with me." He said to him, "O man, who made me one who divides?" He turned to his disciples, he said to them, "I am not one who divides, am I?"

73. Jesus said, "The harvest is great, but the workers are few; but beseech the Lord to send workers to the harvest."

74. He said, "Lord, there are many standing around the cistern, but no one in the cistern."

75. Jesus said, "Many are standing at the door, but the solitary will enter the bridal chamber."

76. Jesus said, "The Kingdom of the Father is like a merchant who had goods; he found a pearl. This was a prudent merchant. He gave up (i.e., sold) the goods, he bought the one pearl for himself. You also must seek for the treasure which does not perish, which abides where no moth comes near to eat, nor worm destroys."

77. Jesus said, "I am the light which is above all of them, I am *the All; the All* came forth from me and *the All* reached me. Split wood, I am there; lift the stone up, you will find me there." (Change "the All" to "all things"?)

78. Jesus said, "Why did you come to the field? To see a reed shaken by the wind? And to see a [man clo]thed in soft clothes?

[Behold, your] kings and your great ones are clothed in soft (clothes) and they [shall] not be able to know the truth."

79.   A woman in the crowd said to him, "Blessed is the womb which bore you and the breasts which fed you." He said to (her), "Blessed are those who have heard the Word of the Father (and) have kept it in truth. For there will be days when you will say: 'Blessed is the womb which has not conceived and the breasts that have not suckled.' "

80.   Jesus said, "He who has known the world has found the body, but he who has found the body, the world is not worthy of him."

81.   Jesus said, "He who has become rich, let him become king, and he who has power, let him renounce it."

82.   Jesus said, "He who is near me is near the fire, and he who is far from me is far from the Kingdom."

83.   Jesus said, "The images are manifest to the man, and the light in them is hidden in the image of the light of the Father. He will reveal himself and his image is hidden by his light."

84.   Jesus said, "When you see your likeness, you rejoice. But when you see your images which came into being before you, (which) do not die nor are manifest, how much you will bear!"

85.   Jesus said, "Adam came into existence from a great power and a great wealth, and he was not worthy of you. For, if he had been worthy, he [would] not [have tasted] death."

86.   Jesus said, "[The foxes have] h[oles] and the birds have [their] nests, but the Son of Man does not have any place to lay his head and to rest."

87.   Jesus said, "The body is wretched which depends on a body, and the soul is wretched which depends on these two."

88.   Jesus said, "The angels and the prophets have come to you and they will give you that which is yours and you give to them what is in your hands, (and) say to yourselves, 'On which day will they come and receive what is theirs?' "

89.   Jesus said, "Why do you wash the outside of the cup? Do you not know that he who made the inside is also he who made the outside?"

90. Jesus said, "Come to me because my yoke is easy and my mastery is gentle and you will find your rest."

91. They said to him, "Tell us who you are so that we can believe in you." He said to them, "You examine the face of the heavens and the earth, and (yet) you have not known him who is in front of your face, nor do you know how to examine this time."

Section Four

92. Jesus said, "Search and you will find, but those things which you asked me in those days, I did not tell you then; now I want to speak them, and you do not ask about them."

93. "Do not give what is holy to the dogs, because they will throw it on the dung heap. Do not throw the pearls to the pigs, lest they become . . . [text uncertain]."

94. Jesus [said], "He who searches, will find . . . it will open to him."

95. Jesus [said], "If you have money, do not lend it at interest, but give [to those] from whom you will not receive it (back again)."

96. Jesus [said], "The Kingdom of the Father is like a woman, she took a bit of leaven, she hid it in dough, she made big loaves. He who has ears let him hear."

97. Jesus said, "The Kingdom of the [Father] is like a woman who was carrying a jar which was full of meal. While she was walking on a distant road, the handle of the jar broke; the meal spilled out behind her onto the road. She did not know; she was not aware of the accident. After she came to her house, she put the jar down; she found it empty."

98. Jesus said, "The Kingdom of the Father is like a man who wanted to kill a powerful man. He drew the sword in his house, he thrust it into the wall so that he would know if his hand would stick it through. Then he killed the powerful one."

99. The disciples said to him, "Your brothers and your mother are standing outside." He said to them, "Those here who do the will of my Father, they are my brothers and mother; they will enter the Kingdom of my Father."

100.   They showed Jesus a gold (coin) and they said to him, "Caesar's men demand taxes from us." He said to them, "Give Caesar's things to Caesar; give God's things to God, and what is mine give to me."

101.   "He who does not hate his [father] and his mother in my way will not be able to be my [disciple] and he who does [not] love his father and his mother in my way, will not be able to be my [disciple], for my mother [according to the flesh gave me death (conjecture: Quispel)], but [my] true [mother] gave me life."

102.   Jesus said, "Woe to them, the Pharisees, for they are like a dog lying in the food-trough of oxen, for he does not eat, nor let the oxen eat."

103.   Jesus said, "Blessed is the man who knows in which part (of the night) the robbers will come, so that he will rise and gather his [. . .] and gird up his loins before they come in. . . ."

104.   They said [to him], "Come, let us pray today and let us fast." Jesus said, "Why? What sin have I committed, or by what (transgression) have I been conquered? But after the bridegroom has left the bridechamber, then let them fast and pray."

105.   Jesus said, "He who acknowledges his father and mother, will be called the son of a harlot."

106.   Jesus said, "When you make the two one, you shall be Sons of Man and when you say, 'Mountain, move away,' it will move."

107.   Jesus said, "The Kingdom is like a man, a shepherd, who had a hundred sheep. One of them, which was the largest, wandered off. He left the ninety-nine; he searched for the one until he found it. After he tired himself, he said to the sheep, 'I love you more than the ninety-nine.' "

108.   Jesus said, "He who drinks from my mouth will be as I am, and I will be he, and the things that are hidden will be revealed to him."

109.   Jesus said, "The Kingdom is like a man who had a treasure [hidden] in his field, and he did not know it. And [after] he died, he left it to his son. His son did not know, he received

the field, he sold [it] and he who bought it, he went, while he was plowing, [he found] the treasure. He began to lend money at interest to [whom] he wished."

110. Jesus said, "He who has found the world and becomes rich, let him deny the world."

111. Jesus said, "The heavens and the earth will roll back in your presence, and he who lives by the Living One will not see death nor. . . ." because Jesus said, "He who finds himself, the world is not worthy of him."

112. Jesus said, "Woe to the flesh which depends on the soul; woe to the soul which depends on the flesh."

113. His disciples said to him, "On what day will the Kingdom come?" (He said,) "It will not come by expectation. They will not say, 'Look here,' or, 'Look there,' but the Kingdom of the Father is spread out on the earth and men do not see it."

A Saying Added Later to the Basic Text

114. Simon Peter said to them, "Let Mary leave us, because women are not worthy of the Life." Jesus said, "Look, I shall guide her so that I will make her male, in order that she also may become a living spirit, being like you males. For every woman who makes herself male will enter the Kingdom of Heaven."

The Gospel according to Thomas

Notes

CHAPTER ONE

1. A. Guillaumont, et al. *The Gospel According to Thomas* (New York: Harper and Row, 1959), and J. Doresse, *The Secret Books of the Egyptian Gnostics* (New York: Viking, 1960).
2. Bertil Gaertner, *The Theology of the Gospel According to Thomas* (New York: Harper and Row, 1961), Robert Grant with David Noel Freedman, *The Secret Sayings of Jesus* (New York: Doubleday, 1960), Johannes Leipoldt, *Das Evangelium nach Thomas* (Berlin: Akademie-Verlag, 1967), H.E.W. Turner and Hugh Montefiore, *Thomas and the Evangelists* (Naperville, Ill.: Allenson, 1962), R. McL. Wilson, *Studies in the Gospel of Thomas* (London: Mobray, 1960). These five are probably the best known compendia of arguments for the gnosticism of the Gospel of Thomas, but there are others.
3. James M. Robinson, ed., *The Nag Hammadi Library* (New York: Harper and Row, 1977).
4. On the fact that the Nag Hammadi texts derive from a Christian monastery, cf. J. Barns, "Greek and Coptic Papyri from the Covers of the Nag Hammadi Codices," in *Essays on the Nag Hammadi Texts in Honor of Pahor Labib*, ed. Martin Krause (Leiden: Brill, 1975) and cf. T. Save-Soderberg, "The Sitz im Leben of the Nag Hammadi Library," in *Les Textes de Nag Hammadi*, ed. J. Menard (Leiden: Brill, 1975) and cf. F. Wisse, "Gnosticism and Early Monasticism in Egypt," in *Gnosis, Festschrift für Hans Jonas*, ed. Barbara Aland (Göttingen: Vandehoeck and Ruprecht, 1978).
5. Turner and Montefiore, *Thomas and the Evangelists*, p. 78.
6. Helmut Koester and James Robinson, *Trajectories Through Early Christianity* (Philadelphia: Fortress Press, 1971), p. 132.
7. Turner and Montefiore, *Thomas and the Evangelists*, p. 62.
8. Gilles Quispel, "Gnosis and the New Sayings of Jesus," *Eranos Jahrbuch*, 1969, vol. 38, p. 269.
9. Ibid., p. 271.

10. Turner and Montefiore, *Thomas and Evangelists*, p. 65.
11. Ibid., p. 69.
12. Koester and Robinson, *Trajectories*, p. 129.
13. Wilson, *Studies*, p. 113.
14. Ibid., pp. 113–114.
15. Kendrick Grobel, "How Gnostic is the Gospel of Thomas?" *New Testament Studies*, Volume 8, 1962.
16. Ibid., p. 373.
17. Ibid.
18. Koester and Robinson, *Trajectories*, p. 132.
19. Ibid.
20. Ibid.
21. Ibid., pp. 179–180.
22. Ibid., pp. 181–182.
23. Joachim Jeremias, *The Parables of Jesus* (New York: Scribner's, 1972), p. 224.
24. Ibid., p. 32–33.
25. Gaertner, *Theology*, p. 238.
26. Wilson, *Studies*, p. 93.
27. Koester and Robinson, *Trajectories*, pp. 71–113.
28. Ibid., p. 102.
29. Ibid., pp. 102–103.
30. Ibid., p. 113.
31. Ibid., p. 135.
32. Ibid., p. 136.
33. Ibid., p. 186.

CHAPTER TWO
1. Wilson, *Studies*, p. 146.
2. Koester and Robinson, *Trajectories*, pp. 127–128.
3. Ibid.
4. Ibid.
5. Ibid., pp. 136–137.
6. Quispel, "Gnosis and New Sayings," *passim*.
7. cf. Stevan Davies, *The Revolt of the Widows: The Social World of the Apocryphal Acts* (Carbondale, Illinois: SIU Press, 1980).
8. Turner and Montefiore, *Thomas and Evangelists*, p. 95.
9. Gerd Theissen, *Sociology of Early Palestinian Christianity* (Philadelphia: Fortress, 1977).
10. Wilson, *Studies*, p. 19.
11. Ibid., p. 11.
12. Robinson, *Nag Hammadi Library*, pp. 346, 454.
13. Gaertner, *Theology*, p. 226.
14. Turner and Montefiore, *Thomas and Evangelists*, pp. 36–37.
15. Ibid., p. 35.
16. Ibid., p. 34.

17. Wilson, *Studies*, p. 27.
18. Ibid., pp. 12–13.
19. Turner and Montefiore, *Thomas and Evangelists*, p. 83.
20. Koester and Robinson, *Trajectories*, p. 139.
21. Ibid., p. 138.
22. Ibid., p. 139.
23. Ibid., p. 186.
24. Ibid., pp. 104–105.
25. Ugo Bianchi, ed., *The Origins of Gnosticism* (Leiden: E. J. Brill, 1970).
26. Robinson, *Nag Hammadi Library*, p. 117.
27. Ibid.
28. Ibid.
29. Ibid.

CHAPTER THREE

1. Gerhard von Rad, *Wisdom in Israel* (Nashville: Abingdon Press, 1972), p. 148.
2. Ibid.
3. Koester and Robinson, *Trajectories*, pp. 172–173.
4. Geza Vermes, *The Dead Sea Scrolls in English* (Harmondsworth, Middlesex: Penguin Books, 1962), pp. 92–93.
5. Ibid., p. 75.
6. David Winston, *The Wisdom of Solomon*, Anchor Bible Series, vol. 43 (New York: Doubleday, 1979), p. 38.
7. Ernst Käsemann, *The Testament of Jesus* (Philadelphia: Fortress Press, 1968), p. 51.

CHAPTER FOUR

1. Martin Hengel, *The Son of God* (Philadelphia: Fortress Press, 1976), p. 75.
2. H. A. Wolfson, *Philo* (Cambridge: Harvard University Press, 1947), p. 238.
3. Gaertner, *Theology*, p. 201.
4. Eduard Lohse, *Colossians and Philemon* (Philadelphia: Fortress Press, 1971), pp. 53–54.
5. Ibid., pp. 54–55.
6. Hengel, *Son of God*, p. 51.
7. von Rad, *Wisdom*, p. 305.

CHAPTER FIVE

1. Lohse, *Colossians*, pp. 50–51.
2. Hengel, *Son of God*, pp. 69, 72.
3. Ibid., p. 57.
4. Ibid., pp. 74–75.

CHAPTER SIX

1. Elisabeth Schüssler Fiorenza, "Wisdom Mythology and the Christological Hymns of the New Testament," in *Aspects of Wisdom in Judaism and Early Christianity*, ed. Robert Wilken (Notre Dame: Notre Dame University Press, 1974), p. 17.
2. James Robinson, "Jesus as Sophos and Sophia," in *Aspects*, ed. Wilken, p. 9.
3. Koester and Robinson, *Trajectories*, p. 186.
4. cf. M. Jack Suggs, *Wisdom Christology and Law in Matthew's Gospel* (Cambridge: Harvard University Press, 1970).
5. Robinson, "Jesus as Sophos," p. 10.
6. Suggs, *Wisdom Christology*, pp. 57, 97. Italics in originals.
7. Lohse, *Colossians*, p. 46.
8. Ibid., p. 48.
9. Raymond Brown, *The Gospel of John: Volume One*, Anchor Bible Series, vol. 29a (New York: Doubleday, 1966), p. 523.
10. Raymond Brown, "The Gospel of Thomas and St. John's Gospel," *New Testament Studies*, vol. 9, p. 157.
11. Ibid., p. 156.
12. Brown, *Gospel of John*, p. cxxiii.
13. Käsemann, *Testament*, p. 53.
14. Brown, *Gospel of John*, p. cxxiii.
15. Ibid.
16. Ibid.
17. Ibid.
18. Ibid.
19. Ibid.
20. Ibid., cxxiii–cxxiv.
21. Käsemann, *Testament*, p. 16.
22. Brown, "Gospel of Thomas," p. 167.
23. Ibid.
24. Ibid.
25. Ibid.
26. Ibid.

CHAPTER SEVEN

1. Jonathan Z. Smith, "The Garments of Shame," *History of Religions*, vol. 5, 1965.
2. Ibid., p. 218.
3. Ibid., p. 221.
4. Ibid., p. 222.
5. Ibid., pp. 224–232.
6. Ibid., pp. 231–232.
7. Ibid., p. 232.
8. Ibid., p. 233.

9. Ibid., p. 232.
10. Ibid.
11. Ibid., p. 236.
12. Ibid.
13. R. Beasley-Murray, *Baptism in the New Testament* (Grand Rapids, Mich.: Eerdmans, 1962), p. 29.
14. Suggs, *Wisdom Christology*, p. 78.
15. Ibid., p. 83.
16. Ibid., p. 84.
17. Ibid.
18. Ibid., pp. 46–47.
19. Raymond Brown, *The Community of the Beloved Disciple* (New York: Paulist Press, 1979), p. 28.
20. Hengel, *Son of God*, p. 55.
21. Wayne A. Meeks, "The Image of the Androgyne: Some Uses of a Symbol in Earliest Christianity," *History of Religions*, vol. 13, 1974, pp. 180–181.
22. Ibid., p. 183.
23. Ibid., p. 185.
24. Quispel, "Gnosis," pp. 286–287.
25. Smith, "Garments," p. 234.
26. Käsemann, *Testament*, p. 69.
27. Meeks, "Androgyne," p. 207.
28. cited in Lohse, *Colossians*, p. 76, n.65.

APPENDIX I

1. Koester and Robinson, *Trajectories*, p. 94, n. 47.
2. John D. Turner, *The Book of Thomas the Contender*, SBL Dissertation Series, vol. 23 (Missoula, Mont.: Scholars Press, 1975), p. 105.
3. Another idea of the organization of the Gospel of Thomas can be found in Philip Meerburg's *De Structuur van het Koptische Evangele Naar Thomas* (Maastricht: Drukkerij Boosten and Stols, 1964). His theory is that the Gospel of Thomas should be divided at the point of questions or significant interruptions. The logia between questions constitute answers to those questions. I find that one must interpret virtually all logia by complex allegories in order to make this scheme work at all. The scholar who originated this theory believes that Thomas is a gnostic document and so tends to hide the deeper meaning of a word. Hence, he is sympathetic to allegorical reading as a technique for understanding.

Index of the Gospel of Thomas, Canonical Scriptures, and Apocrypha